Complete Leadership

From the life and work of Pramukh Swami Maharaj

By

BAPS Family

Dedicated to

Lord Swaminarayan & Gunatit Parampara

Preface

Pramukh Swami Maharaj was a great socio spiritual leader. As a river flows for others; tree never eats its fruits and give it to others; the sun rises to nourish various herbs and plants, provides light and energy to us without any expectations in return; Swamiji lived for others for his entire life on this earth for 95 years. He selflessly served others for his lifetime. He lived every moment what he quoted, "In Joy of others, lies our own. In progress of others, rests our own."

In our daily routine most often, we ignore the most important factors responsible for our existence and life. For example, Sun is vital for the existence of the Earth and our life on it, but we hardly notice it and know a very little about it. We know its single perspective, as a brightening, off-white sphere, shaped to round. Only a few of us know how big and massive it is. In Mt. Abu, India there are famous spots 'Sunrise Point' and 'Sunset Point.' One can view there rising and setting sun to different colors and fascinating aura around it. Same is true for great leaders. They look ordinary, but when we stand on a specific point, we can see many perspectives to guide us in the journey of life. Pramukh Swami Maharaj was a rainbow of many virtues, some books had been published on him with some perspectives, here it is an attempt to highlight the virtue of his leadership.

Swamiji could build more than 1100 temples across the globe. The Marvel creation, 'Akshardham' built at the capital of India in Delhi became a landmark of management and leadership. It's a masterpiece of ancient Indian architecture, and every corner has an inspiring message for people to develop virtues in life. Management Gurus took it as a case study and arranged a series of seminars on it for the biggest temple in the world to complete in mere five years. Many experts said it should have taken 50 years if anyone else other than BAPS did it.

Mr. Mukesh Ambani (CEO, Reliance Industries) said, "My 2000 top management professionals need to learn the project management and leadership from Swamiji." A leading national congress minister Mr. Arun Gujarati said, "A corporate house or even the government cannot lead the Akshardham project to complete within five years. Swamiji is an engineer, a doctor, an advocate, and a very good social reformer. He is an all-around leader." City Development Minister Mr. I.K. Jadeja told Swamiji, "The way you have built this Akshardham in Delhi, I believe every minister must come here and learn leadership and management from you." Mr. Kamlesh Jadav, a construction consultant at Akshardham, reported, "It was an experience of life for me. As a technical person, I experienced the way time, workforce, money and various resources are managed here, I have never seen before and don't believe anyone to manage today."

Guinness book of world records honored him as the 20 most influential people in the world for his services to society. They also awarded him a 'Master Builder' award for building largest number of beautiful temples across the globe. Swamiji served people selflessly. He sacrificed his life and its every moment to please his followers. People loved Swamiji as their leader for his selfless care and love. They loved him for his spotless character and saintliness. Whenever followers in trouble, they approached Swamiji, and he attended them even 2 am at night. In 2007, around 275,000 people got together in Ahmedabad to celebrate his birthday. It was usual that 100,000 devotees come in person on his birthday to greet him. When Swamiji got ill, people would do fasting for up to 4-5 days, barefooted pilgrimage and arrange prayer assemblies for him. He was honored and offered 40 Key to the cities in the US and Australia.

One may surprise that he was the only person in the world whose live notes were taken every moment. The moment he woke up in the morning, a disciple would note his every action, significant words and thought till he slept at night. For 30 years a daily report was written and listened by his followers across the world. It accumulated to more than 36 000 pages written live on him and many books compiled out of it. It shows the importance of his guidance to his followers through his casual actions and talks.

In past 100 years researchers had developed several leadership models like Skills Approach, Situational Leadership, Servant Leadership, Team Leadership, Authentic Leadership, Transformational Leadership etc. This book reveals a new model 'Complete Leadership' from life & work of Pramukh Swami Maharaj. At the core of this model is Common Good, Familyhood and Peace. It effectively defines leadership and simultaneously solves the problem of universal traits of a leader by separating it into 'Basic Leadership Traits' and 'Field Specific Traits'. The model weighs on development of people's seven aspects (1) Personal (2) Intellectual (3) Professional (4) Emotional (5) Social (6) Moral and (7) Spiritual.

In recent years we have understood the importance of transformation of people, moral values and virtues. The Complete Leadership model is in fact not a development of a leadership theory but it's a presentation of a present working solution established by Lord Swaminarayan and his Gunatit successors. It describes how an authentic leader can transform people at large through his inner drive of familyhood, common good and will to serve at its best.

The book is about the development of a human being from bottom to its maximum potential. If one is facing personal problems like addictions, depression or tension then this book may help, if you have family conflicts you may find solutions here, if you are trying to build a team for your noble goal then you have picked up a right choice how to unite people together for a common good cause, if you are running a multinational company and want a useful model for your organizational culture it will help you to a great extent, someone wants to raise the leadership qualities then this book may put him there at peak. The sun is essential for all, and there is no excuse about it, the same way the book is helpful to everyone for their complete development to all aspects of life.

The book is solely written to describe the 'Complete Leadership Model,' and the examples and incidences are put together to understand the model; still, there is a lot not covered here with respect to Swamiji's leadership qualities. This edition is written as an academic work to help students study a new model, so citations are put into the text. This edition is for scholars, teachers, professors and mentors on leadership. I invite them for their valuable inputs and feedback on this model on jkorn612@gmail.com

Contents

1. Pramukh Swami Maharaj ... 9
2. Introduction ... 12
3. Complete Leadership Model ... 15
4. Core of Complete Leadership ... 19
5. Common Traits for Leadership ... 23
6. Goal / Vision ... 25
7. Conceptual ... 27
8. Character / Ethics ... 30
9. Polite ... 44
10. Fearless ... 48
11. Patience ... 51
12. Encouraging/Motivating ... 61
13. Problem Solving / Conflict Management ... 63
13. Familyhood Traits ... 70
15. Personal Care ... 73
16. Responsibility ... 84
17. Sacrifice ... 86
18. Emotional Support ... 92
19. Empathy ... 96
20. Training ... 103
21. Field Specific Traits ... 110
22. Infrastructure ... 115
23. Outcome - Development of People ... 122
24. Personal Development ... 125
25. Intellectual Development ... 129
26. Professional Development ... 131
27. Emotional Development ... 134
28. Social Development ... 136
29. Moral / Ethical Development ... 139
30. Spiritual Development ... 142

31. Implementation 146
32. Complete Leadership Questionnaire 150
33. The Complete Leadership Grid 156
Conclusion 159
Bibliography 160

Complete Leadership

1. Pramukh Swami Maharaj

A Brief Introduction

Pramukh Swami Maharaj was born on 7th December 1921 to Motibhai and Diwaliba in Chansad (a village near Vadodara, Gujarat, India). His childhood name was Shantilal. Shanti means peace. When Shantilal was 1 year old, his parents moved to Rajnagar (a small village in today's Godhra district, Gujarat, India). Shantilal's father, Motibhai was a farmer and his mother, Diwaliba was a housewife.

There were no schools in Rajnagar. Therefore, Shantilal's education started at the age of 9 until they returned to Chansad. There Shantilal studied up to the 5th standard. He was a scholar and always ranked 1st or 2nd. His favorite subjects were History and Math. After the 5th Standard, there was no provision for further studies at Chansad. So, Shantilal went to Padra for his 6th Standard studies.

Shantilal was an honest, religious, brave and talented boy. His multifaceted personality promoted him to leadership roles throughout his childhood. He was a leader of the cricket team at Chansad. He loved peace and was mature enough to settle conflicts and quarrels.

He regularly visited temples and often planned to go to the Himalaya and become a monk. His wish was fulfilled very soon when his spiritual Guruji Shastriji Maharaj invited him through a letter to become a sadhu. On 7th November 1939, Shantilal renounced his family and accepted the entire humanity as his family to serve for the rest of his life. He was initiated by Shastriji Maharaj to the Parshad Diksha on 22nd November 1939 in Ahmedabad, and then Bhagwati Diksha on 10th January 1940 at Gondal, Aksharderi. Then, he was given a monastic name, 'Sadhu Narayanswaroop Das' (Pramukh Swami Maharaj - Life & Work in Brief, 2013).

Narayanswaroopji studied advanced Sanskrit and earned a scholarly title 'Shastri.' Later on, he was engaged in construction activities and social services of BAPS (Bochasanwasi Akshar Purushottam Swaminarayan Sanstha). Shastriji Maharaj trusted him to lead and flourish BAPS. Though there were many senior monks, on 21st May 1950, Shastriji Maharaj appointed him president (Pramukh) of BAPS at the mere age of 28. With deep respect and love, people started calling him 'Pramukh Swami.' After the official ceremony, Pramukh Swamiji washed the utensils and dishes of the devotees after lunch. Someone asked him, "You were appointed the leader; you could have assigned it to others. Why did you do it?" Swamiji replied, "I am always a servant" (Sadhu P. , 2012).

On 23rd January 1971, Pramukh Swamiji became the spiritual head of BAPS. Through his saintliness, efforts, wisdom and leadership skills he put BAPS on the world map in a short span of time. Whatever he did, became a landmark. People accepted his life and work as a perfect model to follow.

When he took charge, BAPS was a tiny organization. It had only 6 temples and around 150 monks. Pramukh Swami Maharaj raised BAPS to new heights. He built more than 1000 temples across the globe and earned a 'Master Builder' award by the Guinness Book of World Records (Pramukh Swami among top 20 in Guiness Book, 2001). The Akshardham temple in Delhi is the largest active Hindu temple in the world. He initiated 1000 monks practicing strict celibacy and abstinence from wealth. Under his leadership, BAPS successfully ran 162 social activities like hospitals, schools, hostels, medical aids, scholarships, relief work and more.

Through 3,850 socio spiritual, cultural centers in India, USA, UK, Europe, Africa, Asia Pacific, and the Middle East he was able to develop each aspect of a person's life. He established an excellent infrastructure of 17,000 weekly assemblies for men, women, youths, teenagers, and children to inspire them for instilling, moral values, peaceful & progressive life, a life free from crime, aggression, and addictions. He developed a volunteer force of 55,000 men and women to serve with devotion and dedication, contributing over 13 million volunteer-hours in serving society annually. Of these, over 10,000 are women volunteers who manage the various moral, cultural, social and spiritual activities for women of all ages (BAPS Swaminarayan Research Institute, n.d.).

Through anti-addiction drives by adult volunteers and children, he could transform hundreds of thousands of people who pledged to give up their dependence on tobacco, drugs, alcohol, gambling and other destructive habits. Swamiji strengthened family unity by advocating daily family assemblies, wherein all family members sit together to pray to God on a daily basis, read Shastras, discuss their day, and understand each other. He nurtured youth talent through training, public performances, and competitions in public speaking, storytelling, scriptural recitations and discourses, drama, traditional dance, vocal and instrumental music, art, crafts, and other activities. He could initiate thousands of children, teenagers, youths, adults and senior citizens throughout North America and Europe take part in Annual National Sponsored Walks to promote family values and raise funds for charitable purposes (Socio Spiritual Works, n.d.).

Swamiji himself lead an austere life, without personal gains or comforts. Despite his age, he traveled from tiny tribal huts to modern metropolitan cities all over the world, to promote morality and spirituality. At his tender word, thousands have left addictions and walked the path of God.

Out of his compassion for humanity, he built over 17,000 villages, town, and city visits and sanctified over 250,000 homes in India and abroad. He had read and replied to over 700,000 letters, and personally counseled over one million people (Pramukh Swami's Work, n.d.).

His remarkable humility, profound wisdom and simplicity touched many. His love for humanity and respect for all religions weaved fabric of cultural unity, interfaith harmony, and universal peace. He sacrificed his life selflessly without any discrimination in service of humanity until he breathed last on 16th August 2016.

2. Introduction

"To remain a credible leader, I must always work first, hardest, and longest on changing myself. This is neither easy nor natural, but it is essential."
~ John C. Maxwell ~

Once a farmer, after plowing the fields was relaxing peacefully at his farm. A youngster from his village was passing by. He had just finished his studies in a megacity and was about to join a well-paying job. On seeing the farmer, he came towards him. The farmer welcomed him as he knew him personally.

Youngster:	You look very relaxed and peaceful.
Farmer:	Yes, I have fulfilled my duties for today.
Youngster:	But, it's just noon. Will you just relax for the rest of the day?
Farmer:	Sure. Why is it strange to you?
Youngster:	I think you should work hard as you have spare time.
Farmer:	Why?
Youngster:	Working more hours will produce more grains.
Farmer:	Then?
Youngster:	Producing more grains will earn you more profits.
Farmer:	Then?
Youngster:	With more profits, you will be able to buy the latest car, new gadgets, and other things.
Farmer:	Then?
Youngster:	You can build a big new house.
Farmer:	Then?
Youngster:	You may furnish it as per your choice, have a big comfortable bed, and relax peacefully on it.
Farmer:	That's what I am doing right now. Why should I ruin my current peace, and gain it again after so much of exercise?

The youth was speechless. Often, people don't know what they need. We need a peaceful life. But we seldom have clarity of it. We keep running because others are running. Steve Jobs had written a letter at his deathbed. The summary is worth a read: "*I reached the pinnacle of success in the business world. In others' eyes, my life is an epitome of success. However, aside from work, I have little joy. Non-stop pursuing wealth will only turn a person into a twisted being, just like me. God gave us the senses to let us feel the love in everyone's heart, not the illusions brought about by wealth. Treasure Love for your family, love for your spouse, love for your friends...Treat yourself well. Cherish others*" (Steve Jobs Last Words Before Death, n.d.).

We are in a race for more production, more profits, the latest technology, and so on. Running, running, running ... then ... regret! The letter is eye-opening for all of us. The legendary success of this century felt that he missed the enjoyment and development of the emotional and social aspects of his life. Mike Tyson could not cope up with moral standards, and he ended up miserable.

We have invented sophisticated vehicles like cars, trains, and planes to save us transportation time. We have smartphones and internet messaging systems to save us communication time. But it's surprising everyone is becoming busier and seem to be running out of time. We are more aware of human relationships than ever before. We have started practicing it in the corporate world. We are trying to treat our employees like family, but at a personal level; the number of divorces is increasing leaving children helpless. We take responsibility to support customers 24 x 7, but we have little time left for our parents. Our speed of technological advancement and knowledge is tremendous, but there is some problem with the direction. We are developing some aspects of life and overlooking certain aspects of it.

There are seven aspects of life: (1) Personal (2) Intellectual (3) Professional (4) Emotional (5) Social (6) Moral and (7) Spiritual. One needs to focus on all these to become self-content and successful. The book reveals a 'Complete Leadership' model to develop all the aspects of life.

Most leadership models have been developed by focusing on past or present leaders. Mahatma Gandhi, Mother Teresa, Martin Luther King, and Abraham Lincoln are a few which come to mind. The past leaders had contributed significantly to leadership styles and models. It's the life and work of great leaders that initiates new leadership models. Robert Greenleaf after reading a book, 'The Journey to the East' discovered the servant leadership model. The 'Complete Leadership' model is carved out of a real success story from the life and work of Pramukh Swami Maharaj, a great socio spiritual leader of this century.

"In the end, you make your reputation and you have your success based upon creditability."

~ Brit Hume ~

3. Complete Leadership Model

"A genuine leader is not a searcher for consensus, but a molder of consensus." ~ Martin Luther King Jr. ~

The 'Complete Leadership' model is, where a leader develops all aspects of the followers or group with an inner drive of common good and peace for all. It focuses on completeness.

Yogiji Maharaj often told a story of an elephant and four blind men. Four blind men lived in a village. Once an elephant entered the village. It was tame and entertained everyone who came to see it. One blind man grasped the elephant's neck and said, "The elephant is like a pestle." The second blind man caught the elephant's tail. He said, "No, the elephant is like a piece of rope." The third blind man found the elephant's ears. He said, "The elephant is like a dustpan." The fourth blind man was holding a leg. He illustrated, "No, no, the elephant is like a pillar." The men described the elephant only with part of the information; they could not describe it completely (101 Tales of Wisdom by Yogiji Maharaj, n.d.). The story falls true in most leadership styles developed till date. The available models focus on some of the aspects of development, not all.

Trait Theory: Galton's Great-man theory implies that the traits which leaders possessed were immutable and could not be developed. (Trait leadership, n.d.). Up to some extent I agree with it, but for some valid reasons, I disagree with it. It is plausible that one can learn leadership traits. Mahatma Gandhi, Nelson Mandela, Martin Luther King, and others learned it. I disagree that it is possible for 'everyone' to learn leadership traits. A seed can thrive in fertile soil. Many people were thrown on the platform for white-black discrimination, but Gandhiji took it very seriously and came up with a mission. Many people read and discussed the books on Gandhiji, but there was a spark to Martin Luther King Jr. and Nelson Mandela. By leader, we mean the best among a group of people. Best are always few. At school or college, there are 20-40 students in a class. The professors and teachers put their best to develop them, but only a few excel to heights. So, it is wise to say that despite everyone; some people can learn leadership traits. We can support Kirkpatrick and Locke who claimed that effective leaders are distinct types of people in several key respects (Northouse, Leadership: Theory and Practice, 2016, p. 20).

Field Specific Leadership Traits: Stogdill, Kirkpatrick, Locke, Mann, Zaccaro, Kemp, and Bader had come up with a list of traits common to a leader (Northouse, Leadership: Theory and Practice, 2016, p. 22). I think generalizing leadership traits is arising conflicts and problems. Researchers have tried to define leadership universal to all fields. However, to be practical, a leader cannot be a universal leader to be successful in all fields. Instead, we should go field specific. Political, Social, Sports, Military, Business, and other fields, each requires a different set of leadership traits. A military leader need not be very emotional or sympathetic. Analyzing world history, we realize that leaders were field specific. Abraham Lincoln was a political leader, Mother Teresa was a social leader and Steve Jobs we term as a business leader. A political leader may not have business leading traits and vice versa. The traits are different for different fields. It is not possible to generalize the leadership traits for all the fields. We can define the set of traits specific to a field. It will ease our job to prepare good leaders.

Skills Approach: This leadership model describes three skills: (1) Technical (2) Human and (3) Conceptual. It is acceptable from skills theory that one needs knowledge and abilities for effective leadership. However, it does not seem possible that everyone can learn all three skills. My perspective is, it is possible for anyone to learn technical skills, but it is not very likely that everyone can learn human skills or conceptual skills to the same degree. It is a pity to hear someone these days saying that they are learning to be emotional. Human skills are a matter of the heart, not the brain or body. Up to some extent, one can learn human skills, but there are person specific limitations with it. For conceptual skills, it seems impossible for everyone to learn. Steve Jobs had a vision. He did not learn it at any university. It is hard to find an institute that claims they can teach conceptual skills to everyone.

It is surprising how a leader can be skillful and not situational, situational and not authentic, authentic and not a servant, servant and not behavioral, behavioral and not a team leader, team leader and not transformational? Different parts make up a car. Four wheels, steering, engine, body, seats, gear, accelerator, brake – all are necessary.

If a mother requires several leadership styles to lead a single kid effectively, then how is it possible for an organization to stick to a single leadership style to lead a large group? A mother requires to be a servant leader to her children. She has to listen, be empathetic, and serve her child with an inner urge 'I must serve my child.'

It is essential for a mother to act as a situational leader to the child. She is caretaker in some situations; she is a cook who prepares food for them; a mother becomes a teacher to start a, b, c, d; she becomes their tennis coach and so on. Whatever their needs are in different situations, the mother copes with it effectively. Sometimes she is supportive and then directive after a child learns it. A mother also shows a behavioral approach. Her concern for the child is always her top priority over results – that is what we desire from a good leader. A mother does not cheat or malpractice with her children – in that sense she is always authentic and trustworthy for her children. Parents worry about their child's bad habits and try to transform them into good habits. Though, not all parents are aware of teaching moral values to their children. Still, some parents teach moral lessons to their children. In this sense, they act as transformational leaders. Every leadership theory has some limitations for its implementation and results. In 'Complete Leadership,' I have tried to eliminate those.

Core: Familyhood, Common Good and Peace			
Basic Leadership Traits	Familyhood Traits	Field Specific Traits	Development of Seven Aspects
1. Goal/Vision 2. Conceptual 3. Character / Ethics 4. Politeness 5. Fearless 6. Patience 7. Encouraging 8. Problem Solving	1. Personal Care 2. Responsibility 3. Sacrifice 4. Emotional Support 5. Empathy 6. Training	1. Conceptual / Service Oriented 2. Knowledge 3. Team Management 4. Media Control 5. Policy 6. Infrastructure	1. Personal 2. Intellectual 3. Professional 4. Emotional 5. Social 6. Moral 7. Spiritual

The Complete Leadership has four sections.

The main section is what I call the Core.

This is about a leader's inner drive. It encompasses a sense of familyhood (Its detailed explanation is under Familyhood Traits), morally common good, and a goal to bring peace and harmony to followers and others.

Familyhood Traits (It's a detailed explanation of core familyhood)

The other three sections lie beneath it.

(1) Basic Leadership Traits

(2) Field Specific Traits

(3) Development of All Aspects

Each of these sections has various characteristics. At last is the outcome of the model. The result and outcome are people developed to all aspects of life.

I have modeled this 'Complete Leadership' model on the life and works of Pramukh Swami Maharaj, and throughout this book, you will find anecdotes, stories, and situations where Swamiji has shown what it is to be a complete leader.

> *"The very essence of leadership is that you have to have vision.*
> *You can't blow an uncertain trumpet."*
> *~ Theodore M. Hesburgh ~*

4. Core of Complete Leadership

"People who are truly strong lift others up. People who are truly powerful bring others together."

~ Michelle Obama ~

t the core of complete leadership has three values. (1) Common Good (2) Familyhood and (3) Peace.

Common Good

In the last 100 years, managers are differentiated from leaders. A common understanding is managers do things right; leader does the right things. It implies that the leadership definition must incorporate the word 'Common Good.' Surprisingly, I found almost each leadership definition stands true more or less on Adolf Hitler and Bin Laden as well. We need to separate pseudo leaders from good leaders in leadership definition. So, here I have added common good to the complete leadership model. 'Common Good' was the inner drive found in every action and thought of Pramukh Swami Maharaj. Someone asked Pramukh Swami Maharaj, "Which thought constantly comes to your mind?" Swamiji said, "Any harm happens to anyone (even my enemy) - this thought never comes to my mind." His motto of life was, "In the joy of others lies our own. In progress of others rests our own" (Pramukh Swami Maharaj:Quotes, n.d.). A leader should think good for all. It's very near to the seventh habit of Stephen Covey 'Think Win-Win.' Still, it makes a difference. Suppose, there are only two mobile phone carrier companies in a country. Both of them unite with a 'Win-Win' condition. They can entertain higher charges from the public and fulfill their means of profits. Here, though they practiced 'Win-Win' but the motive is not common good.

Every leader's motive should aim at common good along with their primary goal/vision. Ethical leadership terms it as 'Altruism.' Sometimes a leader thinks good of the community they belong to or the organization they belong to, but their actions and results harm others. Common good means it should be good for followers and others as well.

Sense of Familyhood

The Oxford Dictionary defines familyhood as, "The relationship between family members; the state of belonging to or being a family." So, familyhood is about feelings, sacrifice, support, responsibility, and attachment we have for our family members. Surprisingly, it's the root cause behind any other popular leadership model like servant leadership, situational leadership, skills leadership, emotional leadership, and others also.

Familyhood can be explained through an example of a family. Think of a family with four members: mother, father, son, and daughter. Now we focus on the mother's role regarding servant leadership. Servant leadership illustrates ten characteristics of a servant leader (Blanchard & Broadwell, Servant Leadership in Action). These ten characteristics are displayed in a mother. Suppose, the mother had a six-month-old baby. The baby cannot talk. Still, the mother can **listen** to his needs. When the baby cries she gets hurt due to **empathy**, she **heals** the baby in case of injury, **serves** while he is ill, has a **vision** for her baby of what she wants him to become, mother is **self-aware** to put aside her personal biases while serving the baby, **steward** as she manages all the resources for the betterment of the child, she had a **foresight** or sixth sense for kid's care, she is committed for its growth and **builds a community** at her home though limited to her husband and children. Thus, a mother proves herself as a servant leader.

A mother serves her children but doesn't serve the neighbor's child with the same empathy. Why? She has a sense of familyhood with her child and family. For neighbors, she possesses less or not at all. It proves that behind servant leadership, the root cause is familyhood. People serve those only; they share a common cause of attachment with. These days, there is much discussion about emotional leadership, that also has its roots in familyhood. The mother has emotions; her emotional intelligence is very high with her child, but it doesn't work for the neighbor's child. What does it mean? An emotionally intelligent person is not emotional to others as a sense of familyhood is missing for others. If the feeling of familyhood is weak, then one can't serve or lead even his/her own family. In the behavioral approach of leadership concern for people is more important than the concern for a result (Northouse, Leadership: Theory and Practice, 2016, p. 76). If a person has the feeling of familyhood, then concern for people will rise automatically. Parents show more concern for their children far more than results. Parents care for their children's emotions over other materialistic gains. So familyhood works behind our behavior. Now if we come to the Situational Approach, the theory holds that a leader should be able to act differently in different situations with followers according to its needs (Leadership Models, n.d.). A mother plays different roles (mother, mentor, servant, teacher, cook, caretaker, security, etc.) in different situations for a child. Thus, familyhood is the root cause to motivate a person to adopt situational leadership with followers in different situations.

The difference between leaders and non-leaders is of how small or large their sense of familyhood is! Gandhiji thought the entire nation as his family. When he saw poor people, who were deprived of a basic necessity of clothing, it hurt Gandhiji deep in his heart. He thought if the people of my nation don't have enough clothes to wear, how can I be fully clothed? He started wearing a loincloth from 22nd September 1921 (What made Gandhiji wear only Loincloth or Dhoti, n.d.).

The great leaders were able to cross the limit of an ordinary person's sense of familyhood and jumped to a higher level where they could see a large group as their family. Mother Teresa was an ordinary woman. Every mother takes care and serves her sick child. But Mother Teresa could extend her sense of familyhood to a large number of sick people, and though she didn't opt for it, she became a leader.

Gandhiji didn't start the independence movement to become a leader. In 1893, when he was thrown on the platform (Pietermaritzburg railway station, n.d.), his inner brotherhood for an entire nation awakened, and he made a difference to history. Martin Luther King belonged to the black community. His keen sense of community brotherhood led him to initiate a great movement against discrimination of racism. It's the limited or extended sense of familyhood or brotherhood which either makes great  leaders or mediocre leaders. These great leaders never studied any leadership style, never attended a seminar on personal development - still they made a difference. They just broadened their periphery of loved ones to cover beyond their family of only 5 or 6 people. If we want to make a difference with family, workplace or community, then it requires us to adopt a higher level of familyhood. If we imply that managers work through their brain and leaders work through their heart, then it's a feeling of familyhood that is essential for any leader. So, familyhood makes a significant difference.

We can't feed water to each leaf, but if we pour water to the root - it reaches every leaf and the tree flourishes. Cultivating a sense of familyhood is feeding water to the root. It can bloom the tree of leadership. Surprisingly, we have leadership traits within us. Adding a single neutron to uranium creates tremendous nuclear energy. In the same way, adding to our familyhood can produce great results.

Peace

Here peace is concerned with peace of mind, calmness, a state above happiness and pleasure. A person feels happy when their desires are fulfilled whether good or bad. One can feel pleasure harassing others. Here peace is different. A person feels peace as an outcome of a common good. It differs from happiness. When a terrorist assassinates others, he is happy to fulfill his job, but can't feel peace at heart. This is what Pramukh Swamiji said in the town of Limbadi on 5th October 2002. He said,

"One who harms others can't be peaceful" (Vicharan Report 2002). On 12th November 2001 in Gondal, Swamiji said, "Peace is to live and let live" (Vicharan Report January 2001). Today we are facing terrorism, gender-based conflicts, cultural groupism in organizations and nations. It's a prime necessity that the leaders account on peace as an outcome."

In Indian scriptures, peace is described as a state of self-realization (Swami ni Vaato, 2/77, n.d.). There is no desire left. It's a stage beyond ups and downs of happiness and sorrow. A person feels complete within. One can achieve this stage after spiritual enlightenment (Bhagwad Geeta, 4/39). Prophets and spiritually pure holy leaders rest in this state. They are not disturbed by external conditions and situations. It's the highest stage of human development. Materialistic success or technology advancements cannot put us in this state. Once again, we can remind Steve Job's regret here. He sought everything but couldn't find peace at last. He missed spiritual development. Complete leadership is a journey towards completeness.

"Leadership is the ability to guide others without force into a direction or decision that leaves them feeling empowered and accomplished.

Complete Leadership

~ Lisa Cash Hanson ~

5. Common Traits for Leadership

"A genuine leader is not a searcher for concensus but a molder of consensus."
~ Martin Luther King Jr. ~

In the past 100 years, several leadership theories have been developed to differentiate Leaders from Non-Leaders. One of them is the Trait Theory It holds that leadership traits are innate in leaders and one cannot learn it. Some of the theories like Situational Approach and Skills Approach hold that one can learn leadership skills (Northouse, Leadership: Theory and Practice, 2016). Many researchers have tried to define a universal set of traits common to leaders. There is a long debate over these characteristics, and so far, there is no defined set of characteristics as an acceptable solution.

Generalizing leadership traits had led to a lot of confusion. Researchers have tried to define leadership traits universal to all fields. But leadership traits can't be universal. However, to be practical, a leader cannot be a universal leader to be successful in all fields. Instead, we should go field specific. Political, Social, Sports, Military, Business; each requires a different set of leadership traits. A military leader need not be too emotional or sympathetic. Analyzing world history, we realize that leaders were field specific. Abraham Lincoln was a political leader. Mother Teresa was a social leader, and Steve Jobs was a business leader. A political leader may not have business leading traits and vice versa. The traits are different for different fields. It is not possible to generalize the leadership traits for all the fields. There can be some traits common for all and others may be field specific.

Expecting all the leadership traits from a person is like expecting someone expert in all the Olympic games with equal talent and skillset. It's impossible. We cannot develop a universal vehicle to run on the road, sail on the sea and fly in the sky with equal comfort and ease. As per the field, the vehicle must have some specific features, with some shared fundamentals common to all. While I was learning software programming, I learned object-oriented programming. There, one can define an object 'A' with basic properties. Other objects B, C, D can be inherited from object A. Now B, C, and D will possess all the properties of object A; plus, some specific properties of their own. According to this reference in our case, essential personal leadership traits are object A, and field-specific traits are object B, C, D and so on. Like in the case of vehicles, all vehicles require an engine, fuel tank – these are common properties (Object A). Now sea sailing vehicles like a boat have a propeller, and road vehicles have tyres. Here both vehicles share some common principles and have some specific characteristics.

In the same way in the Complete Leadership model, traits of leaders are divided into two categories. (1) Common Traits and (2) Field Specific Traits/Skills.

Basic Leadership Traits: Kirkpatrick and Locke who claimed that effective leaders are distinct types of people in several key respects (Northouse, Leadership: Theory and Practice, 2016, p. 20). These are the common traits of any leader. The common traits of any leader are Character, Goal/Vision, Conceptual skills, Politeness, Fearlessness, Patience, Encouraging, and Problem Solving/Conflict Management.

"A leader is the one who knows the way, goes the way, and shows the way."

~ John C. Maxwell ~

6. Goal / Vision

"Setting goals is the first step in turning the invisible into the visible."
~ Tony Robbins ~

A leader without a goal is a journey without a destination. Non-leaders keep changing their goals and principles; while a leader is one who sets the goal and works hard to achieve it. The distractions can't deviate a leader from a decided goal. A leader is always strictly focused on the goal irrespective of failures or delay.

Conceptual skills are the ability of a leader to work with ideas and concepts. Conceptual skills are central to creating a vision and strategic plan for an organization. Conceptual skill has to do with the mental work of shaping the meaning of organizational or policy issues - understanding what a company stands for and where it is or should be going (Northouse, Leadership: Theory and Practice, 2016, p. 48).

Leadership studies also emphasize on goal statement of any organization. A leader should have clarity of the goal/vision. The leader should also be able to communicate his vision to his followers effectively so that it becomes their vision. They must not compromise with organizational principles and goal statement. One significant leadership practice advocates that a leader should write the vision and goal of the organization and ask their employees to read it at regular intervals to align them with their goal statement. Jeff Bezos's vision for Amazon is to make it the most customer-centric company in the world. Southwest Airlines aimed at 'Serve' their clients best. It is for all to see; how successful these companies are today with a focus on their goals with clarity and not compromising on their organizational principles.

Therefore, a goal statement is a must. It keeps the leader and followers on track. It helps them develop and move in a definite direction. It keeps them focused on what they want to become and for why they are here. An effective leader is very conscious and aware of it. His every decision and activity are in tune with the goal. Gandhiji's mission was to gain independence through the path of non-violence. He stuck to it till the very end.

Swamiji's goal statement is reflected in his passport. In the occupation field, he wrote, "Worship God and help people for the same." After the mega project of Akshardham in Delhi was completed, Dr. Subramanyam asked Swamiji, "What is your next project?" Swamiji modestly replied, "Our Guru Shashtriji Maharaj and Yogiji Maharaj have given us a project for a lifetime. That is to worship God and serve people. The mandirs are built along with it."

We can learn from Swamiji how he pursued his goal and was devoted to it. On 31st August 2011, Swamiji was in Mumbai. There was a discussion in an article published in the newspaper whether sadhus should participate in politics? Some sadhus from other sects supported it. Swamiji said, "Sadhu has to live a spiritual, moral life, and inspire people for the same. For a sadhu, there is no need to participate in politics."

Once Bhagwatcharan Swami said to Swamiji, "If you become prime minister, appoint me as your finance minister." Swamiji smiled and said, "We are sadhus. It's not our job. Our job is to help people uplift their morale and serve them."

Swamiji was obvious and firm to his goal and vision. His was a socio-spiritual organization, and he was never going to compromise the integrity and sanctity of it.

"Discipline is the bridge between goals and accomplishment."

~ Jim Rohn ~

7. Conceptual

"Changes call for innovation, and innovation leads to progress."
~ Li Keqiang ~

A leader needs to improve to cope with the surrounding advancements and changes continuously. Keeping his goal intact he introduces new concepts to stay in tune with their followers. Conceptual ability is an essential trait for a leader to sustain and maintain the pace. Pramukh Swamiji had these characteristics.

The Impression of a mandir was of just a place of worship before. Pramukh Swami Maharaj revolutionized this impression. Honorable Prime Minister Narendra Modi said, "Swamiji was a man of vision. I visited the London mandir. I was surprised to see a gymnasium and sports facility for youth on the mandir campus. But today, I realize that to pour cultural values in youth, to attract them to mandirs, it was a visionary step." Swamiji amalgamated two ends - spirituality and social activities. He developed mandirs to become the epicenter of social activities and the backbone of cultural and moral values. His conceptualization skills turned mandirs to shape and nurture society.

In India, not even a Bollywood director had dared to produce a large format film till 2005. Swamiji wished to produce it. Everyone was cautious, "As an NGO, how can we can pull it off? We don't have any experience producing even a regular film or a TV episode." But Swamiji was confident enough to finish it successfully. The large format film finished in record time and won several international awards. It was a novel idea, Swamiji used the latest technology to present spiritual values so effectively at Akshardham. He could move ahead in sync with the modern world while keeping the cultural, moral and spiritual values intact.

Most organizations build their offices and mega buildings through their organizational funds. Swamiji changed this concept. Of the 1000 mandirs, 95% of them have been built of local funds and volunteer services.

Conceptualization refers to an individual's ability to be a visionary for an organization, providing a clear sense of its goals and direction. This characteristic goes beyond day-to-day operational thinking to focus on the "big picture."

BAPS was building the mandirs as per the traditional trends. It was a time when the organization was tiny with limited budget and resources. But Pramukh Swamiji had a 'big picture' in his mind and heart which turned into reality with the first ever Akshardham at Gandhinagar. Jonathan Swift said, *"Vision is the art of seeing what is invisible to others."* Ishwarcharn Swamiji (Convener, BAPS) had a similar experience. He shares one of his most exceptional experiences with Swamiji and the Gandhinagar Akshardham project. He Said, "It is Swamiji's encouragement and inspiration we see Gandhinagar's Akshardham success and glory today. At first, the plan was to build a memorial pillar. Then we came up with an RCC building plan but Swamiji, on the other hand, had different plans in his mind. He submitted his view that a sturdy stone structure to build in the best possible way, one which would serve as a memorial to Bhagwan Swaminarayan for thousands of years. Swamiji kept enhancing our initial idea and evolved it by time to the current edifice. Right until the end, we were still apprehensive: "How will it all end up?", "What will it be like?" (Divine Memories - 1, 1997, p. 4).

Pramukh Swamiji was a visionary leader. He could turn the impossible into possible. He could make dreams come true. He could bring imaginations to reality. One can see his visionary skills in the development of BAPS and its world-class cultural centers in various parts of the world. After Gandhinagar, Swamiji built another Akshardham 4 times in size in New Delhi. It has been mentioned in the Guinness Book of World Records for being the biggest temple. Acquiring 100 acres of land was a dream, but Swamiji acquired it after patience, and an effort lasting 32 years. No one thought of such a magnificent monument before. It became a legend when it only took five years to build. A prominent architect Dr. Satish Gujaral (Renowned Artist and Architecture) on his visit to Akshardham on 27th October 2005 said, "It might take 5 years to plan the way everything is put nicely here, and you have astonished everyone by building it within 5 years" (Kpdas, Pramukhcharitramrut Sagar Part 10, 2009). Warren Bennis quotes, "Leadership is the capacity to translate vision into reality" (Vision Quotes, n.d.).

8th November 2004, Delhi. Sompura Bachubhai was overjoyed expressing the same feelings with tears in his eyes and said, "Till date, we believed the designs we drew on paper, was not possible to carve a 100 percent on stone. In history it happened for the first time we had the designs on paper perfectly carved as it is on the stones. It is only Pramukh Swami Maharaj who did it. Usually, it takes four generations to finish such a mammoth task. One can't finish it in even 60 years, what Pramukh Swamiji finished in just 4 years. I believe Pramukh Swamiji as GOD." (Kpdas, Pramukhcharitramrut Sagar Part 9, 2009).

"Innovation distinguishes between a leader and a follower."

~ Steve Job ~

8. Character / Ethics

"Most people say that it is the intellect which makes a great scientist. They are wrong: it is the character."
~Einstein~

Various leadership theories based on trait approach had listed the leadership traits. Mann has listed six traits necessary in a leader, Stogdill had listed 8 traits, Kirkpatrick and Locke had 7. Zaccaro, Kem, and Bader in 2004 listed 11 characteristics of a leader (Northouse, Leadership: Theory and Practice, 2016, p. 22). The various lists miss the vital trait 'Character.' The character is the hidden part of an iceberg and the base of the outer part of actions (Blanchard & Broadwell, Servant Leadership in Action). The character is the most promising factor for followers to trust the leader. Skills influence the followers of that particular field, but character influences everyone. It's an essential characteristic for a leader. If it is present, it will bring other skillful followers to accomplish the organizational tasks. It can establish a permanent relationship between leader and followers. The character is the base for long-term trustworthy relationships. Gandhiji's influence over the world is due to his character - faith in truth & non-violence. His success didn't depend on his skills, but more so on his character. There were many other leaders far more politically and intellectually skillful than him. However, it was his character and common good motive which united people under him. We may find all other leadership characteristics in notorious leaders as well. It's only character and a motive for the common good that makes a difference between leaders and non-leaders.

The current acting president and spiritual head of BAPS, HDH Mahant Swami Maharaj spoke about character. He said, "True character is like gold. No matter how much one decorates and adorns brass, it can never become gold. Similarly, deceit and fraud can never take the place of pure character." (Kjdas, 1997).

Pramukh Swami Maharaj was able to spread BAPS to 45 countries due to his spotless character. People trusted him, helped him, joined him, obeyed each word – the most reasonable cause behind it was Swamiji's genuine character. Followers knew he would not harm them or do anything wrong to build a wall of mistrust. We need first to work out why do people do wrong to others? The root cause is greed for wealth, lust, unfulfilled desires, and ego. If we examine world history involving family conflicts, social conflicts, organizational conflicts, national or international conflicts, and any other conflict, the very root cause is ego, greed for wealth & lust. One who is free from these can be a true leader. Nelson Mandela, Gandhiji, Mother Teresa, and other great leaders of the world could serve the masses through their leadership due to their abstinence from these three root causes.

Pramukh Swamiji Maharaj practiced celibacy his entire life. He never earned, touched, or kept money in any form in any account. Dr. APJ Abdul Kalam quotes, "Those who are spiritually pure can serve better." Swamiji could serve everyone selflessly without any desire for returns or profits because his ego-free personality was the highest of the spiritual purity. We can see some of the incidences here. (Pramukh Swami Maharaj A Living Philosopher , n.d.).

Celibacy

Mahatma Gandhi wrote in his autobiography that when he was about 34 years old, he heard the Inner Voice saying that the observance of total celibacy was indispensable for further spiritual progress. Gandhiji was already doing selfless service, observing fasts, kept mum on Sundays, daily praying, and reading the *Bhagavad Gita*. But later he was convinced: "Further progress is not possible unless I practice complete celibacy." Gandhiji then consulted his wife Kasturba, who agreed to his proposal. He was 34 or 35 years old and from that age until 79, for more than 40 years, he observed strict celibacy (Teachings, n.d.). Gandhiji could not serve the highest order without this discipline. He concluded, "Those who want to perform national service, or to have a gleam of the real religious life, must lead a celibate life, whether married or unmarried" (The Ashram Vows, n.d.).

Despite Pramukh Swami Maharaj's traveling in India and abroad, he has never compromised in the observance of the moral and spiritual commands prescribed by Bhagwan Swaminarayan. In consonance with our Hindu Shastras, Bhagwan Swaminarayan has prescribed 5 moral vows for his sadhus. One of those principle vows is eight-fold celibacy (Moral Disciplines, n.d.).

On 26th December 1977, Pramukh Swami Maharaj met the President of Tanzania, Julius Nyerere, at his residence. The president was impressed by Swamiji's profound saintliness and divinity. He asked Swamiji to bless his 90-year-old mother who was ill. Swamiji explained that because of his vow of brahmacharya he could not personally bless his mother, but he would pray and bless her from far and his blessings would reach her and make her well. The president was convinced of Swamiji's purity and his blessings (Kpdas, Pramukhcharitramrut Sagar Part 3, 2009).

Many social workers and leaders have requested Pramukh Swami Maharaj to allow his sadhus a little liberty in their vow of celibacy by permitting them to talk to women who would subsequently enhance the spread of the organization. To this Swamiji answers that he does not believe in the spread of the organization at the cost of sacrificing their moral vows. If the organization spreads then, it would be right, and if it doesn't then, he would not be worried.

Warren Bennis said, "Managers get things right, leaders do the right thing" (Bennis, 1998). Swamiji was a monk and as per the organization's vows, practiced strict celibacy. A renowned national educationalist forcefully insisted Swamiji to give up celibacy vow for the organization's growth. Swamiji boldly told him, "If the organization doesn't grow, let it be small. I must stick to our vows and ethical standards." At the same time, other organizations were growing. Swamiji could have compromised with his vows and spread the institution, but he didn't. He maintained the ethical standards to its glory and continued developments staying within his moral boundaries. Here we see the difference between a manager and leader! In the long run, people loved him for his long-term promises and ethics.

In 1980, Swamiji was touring UK and USA as part of the Bicentenary of Lord Swaminarayan which was to take place in 1981 in India. When Swamiji was in London in June-July, he was suffering from cataract. His vision was blurry. The situation worsened as Swamiji continued his rigorous tour of the USA. At one stage, it had gotten so worse to the point that it became impossible for Swamiji to identify his slippers which he had taken off to enter the temple for darshan.

As soon as the saints and devotees realized Swamiji's plight, they arranged for an immediate eye check-up in Boston. It was later discovered that Swami's eyes were so affected that if the check-up had been delayed a few weeks, there was grave danger of Swamiji losing his eyesight forever. The eye specialist in Boston, Dr. Hutchinson, advised an immediate operation of the left eye. Everything was arranged, but one issue remained unsettled.

"Who is going to treat me in the hospital?" asked Swamiji.

"Well, the nurses," came a reply.

But how could females attend to Swamiji? Won't this infringe with his vow of celibacy? The sadhus informed Dr. Hutchinson about this, but he said, "Of course, the female nurses have to assist in the operation. It is impossible to find male nurses."

Swamiji said, "I can't give up the vow of celibacy. Let me lose my eyes" (Divine Memories - 1, 1997, p. 43).

It's all very well keeping to the rules in the ordinary course of one's life. But Swamiji had held firm his celibacy even in extreme time of trials. And it is only during such circumstances that a person's real character shines through – because, in the absence of wind, even a heap of cotton is as reliable and stable as a mountain-top.

Free of Avarice

It's astounding that Swamiji was leading a worldwide organization, regularly traveled for 72 years, ran 162 social-spiritual activities, built 1000 mandirs and Akshardham, and still never kept a single penny with him. He had no pocket, no wallet, no bank account or any other wealth to his name.

Once Swamiji was traveling from Ahmedabad to Mumbai by train. The ticket checker came to him and demanded the reservation charges. Swamiji and his fellow sadhus had tickets but not a single penny with them to pay for reservation charges. That day, the president of BAPS was helpless before the TC. A co-passenger saw this pitiful state and paid the Rs.50 reservation charges to the TC. The people around were surprised to know that Swamiji never touches or keep money and doesn't possess any property or balance in the bank (Sadhuta na Sumeru, 1995).

Swamiji traveled to many countries, but he kept this vow. The airport authority in Tanzania experienced it. Some spiteful person had spread rumors that the group of Sadhus with Pramukhswami traveling to Daresalam (Tanzania) are carrying diamonds. The customs officer ordered a strict search of the luggage despite a request from the devotees. After a thorough search, they did not find any diamond, not even permissible currency of 75 Shilling per passengers. The customs officer with surprise and regret informed that during his life, he has never come across such people (Moksha nu Dwar Satpurush, 1995, p. 59). Swamiji was the first ever president of an organization who was not paid, had a zero balance and zero property for his entire life.

As Swamiji abstained from greed, lust, and ego, there was no cause left to do wrong to anyone for anything. He once said, "May something happen ill to anyone –

this thought never came to my mind even once." Terrorists attacked Swamiji's most beautiful creation, the 'Akshardham' at Gandhinagar. Commandos shot them dead. When Swamiji arrived there, he offered flowers to the deceased terrorists and prayed for their salvation. One who prays and offer flowers to his enemies, how can he commit anything ill? Reading Gandhiji's incidences inspired Martin Luther King, Jr. and Nelson Mandela. They acquired strength from his actions and character.

Egoless Saint

An article on the Harvard Business Review website says, "An unchecked ego can warp our perspective or twist our values." In the words of Jennifer Woo, CEO and chair of The Lane Crawford Joyce Group, Asia's largest luxury retailer, "Managing our ego's craving for fortune, fame, and influence is the prime responsibility of any leader." When we're caught in the grip of the ego's craving for more power, we lose control. Ego makes us susceptible to manipulation; it narrows our field of vision; and it corrupts our behavior, often causing us to act against our values" (Ego is the enemy of Good Leadership, 2018).

Because our ego craves positive attention, it can make us susceptible to manipulation. It makes us predictable. When people know this, they can play to our ego. When we're a victim of our own need to be seen as significant, we end up being led into making decisions that may be detrimental to ourselves, our people, and our organization.

An inflated ego also corrupts our behavior. When we believe we're the sole architects of our success, we tend to be ruder, more selfish, and more likely to interrupt others. This is especially true in the face of setbacks and criticism. In this way, an inflated ego prevents us from learning from our mistakes and creates a defensive wall that makes it difficult to appreciate the rich lessons we glean from failure.

A leader's ego can ruin the entire organization and even nation. Ego is a superintendent; it brings an army of envy, anger, hatred, and many other evils (Sarangpur-8: The Characteristics of Jealousy, n.d.). It has the potential to harm an organization's emotional climate. Daniel Goleman in Primal Leadership has mentioned that in a study of nineteen insurance companies, the climate created by the CEOs among their direct reports predicted the business performance of the entire organization: In 75 percent of the cases, climate alone accurately sorted companies into high versus low profits and growth.

A leader is also a model for their followers. A leader's humble and egoless behavior can enhance the climate and inspire the followers to practice the same.

Swamiji's egoless stand resolved conflicts and created a favorable climate. Atmaswaroopdas Swami describes it as follows,

"The year was 1980 in London. The devotees wished to organize a special outing with Swamiji to spend some time with him. The picnic was arranged at Epping Forest. Devotees had gathered in large numbers to make the most of this opportunity. It was planned such that, Swamiji would complete a few visits to devotee's homes, and on the way before going to Epping Forest. The assembly had started at Epping Forest.

While the home visits were in full swing, some devotees insisted that Swamiji visit their homes too. This was not planned, nor scheduled for. Swamiji fulfilled their wish. At Epping Forest, everyone including some BBC reporters was eagerly waiting for Swamiji. The reporters were hoping to cover the assembly for their *India Dances, and Festivities* show. But soon, the reporter's patience ran out, and they left.

Swamiji arrived half an hour later. As soon as he sat down in the assembly, it started raining heavily, the assembly dispersed and Swamiji went inside a nearby school hall. Everyone's expectations and the excitement of the trip dampened. They were supposed to spend the whole day with Swamiji. But it was not to be as the senior devotees had taken Swamiji on visits. Being hurt, some criticized the seniors amongst themselves. "They should've known. No visits should have been kept in the first place... We had just about managed to get the BBC to come, and even they left... Nobody cares about us..." By evening, these words of criticism had reached Swamiji.

The next day at the assembly in Islington, Swamiji began his discourse with an apology. "Sorry. Firstly, I would like to apologize for yesterday. It was my fault. I am to blame for arranging the extra visits and thus turning up late for the assembly. It's no one else's fault – so please, forgive me." Swamiji's words were so full of love and regretted that every single devotee's heart was pierced. The critics realized their mistake in airing their disappointment in public. Those who (in fact) had organized the extra visits in the first place were stunned to hear Swamiji bear the blame for their mistake. Many shed tears of regret in the assembly that morning (Divine Memories - 1, 1997, p. 40).

"A good leader takes a little more than his share of the blame, a little less than his share of the credit."

~ Arnold H. Glasow ~

A leader has to deal with a variety of people, of different temperaments and their opposing views. Being an egoist may create conflicts. Consequently, it may cost time, money, reputation, and relations. Egoists can't serve or lead for long. The more a person conquers the ego, the more he can serve and may turn rivals into friends.

In 1986 in Mumbai, Swamiji was resting at a devotee's house after an operation to remove a benign tumor in his right thigh. One day, an officeholder and well-educated friend of the host arrived. On seeing Swamiji, old prejudices surfaced, and he was overwhelmed with rage. He began to throw wild accusations in a stinging tone at Swamiji. Even an ordinary person could appreciate the condition of an ill person, but here was a respectable man who was behaving quite outrageously. Swamiji let him vent his anger and did not say a word in defense. Not only that, Swamiji stopped a sadhu who was correcting the offender's indecency. In the end, Swamiji's sweet silence overpowered the bitter onslaught. Blessing Ingratitude: The story does not end here.

Two years later, the same man came to see Swamiji for some work. Swamiji got up from his seat in the assembly, welcomed him with a garland and offered him a seat on stage. When C.M. Patel, Chairman of the UK Satsang activities, arrived, Swamiji again got up from his seat and introduced him to the man. Furthermore, Swamiji announced in the assembly the purpose of the man's visit and asked everyone present to give their support and co-operation to him. The fascinating thing was that at that time, the man was not holding any office at all (Kpdas, Pramukhcharitramrut Sagar Part 6, 2009).

> *"The first human who hurled an insult instead of a stone was the founder of civilization." ~Sigmund Freud~*

There was a particular individual in the habit of criticizing Swamiji. He often visited homes of devotees and spoke ill of Swamiji. Many knew of his malicious intent. One day when Swamiji was in Ahmedabad, there were special delicacies for lunch. The critic was sitting in the dining hall. Atmaswarup Swami and other sadhus were serving the food. Gesturing with his eyes, Swamiji called Atmaswarup Swami and instructed him, "Serve that man lovingly." Swamiji was compassionate upon all.

In 1982 at Heathrow Airport, London, Dadubhai Patel had come right up to the plane to greet Swamiji in his Rolls Royce. With Dadubhai chauffeuring, Swamiji sat in the passenger seat. Three sadhus and C.M. Patel took their places in the back. There was no room for the guide that had come with Dadubhai. The question arose of how to find a way out of such a busy airport without someone who was familiar with the roads. Dadubhai presented the problem to Swamiji and politely asked him to sit on the gearbox. Without delay, Swamiji moved over and called in the guide to sit in his seat and gave directions. The Rolls Royce had come to welcome Swamiji, but he was sitting on the gearbox, while a navigator sat in his place (Anandswaroopdas, 1998)!

On 25th January 1974, Pramukh Swami Maharaj departed with nine sadhus amid a joyous farewell for his first Satsang tour abroad since becoming a guru in 1971. The plane took off from Mumbai at 10.15 am and landed in Nairobi at 1.22 pm. All the passengers disembarked, but Pramukh Swami Maharaj and the sadhus were ordered to stay aboard. Then at 4.15 pm, without any reason, they were instructed to fly back to Mumbai. Everyone in the group was saddened by the unexpected order to return. But Swamiji was as happy and calm as before like nothing happened at all (Kpdas, Pramukhcharitramrut Sagar Part 3, 2009).

Swamiji's egoless personality was natural. One could read it without any words. When Dr. Kurian met Swamiji for the first time, Viveksagar Swamiji started talking about Swamiji's egoless personality. Dr. Kurian said, "You need not to tell it, his eyes tell all." Swami Harinarayananand, the president of the National Sadhu Samaj, said, "I have never seen such a personality as Swamiji, so egoless" (Kpdas, Pramukhcharitramrut Sagar Part 3, 2009).

Only an egoless person can forget and forgive the unfortunate events and people. That creates a positive and conflict-free favorable climate and culture in an organization or community. Mahant Swami Maharaj said, "There is a difference of a single letter between 'Power' and 'Powder,' the letter' stands for the dust of ego. Those who can kick it off the atmosphere enjoys the power of real leadership (Kjdas, 1997).

One man had been staying in the organization's mandirs for years but had a very hot temper. He had a self-imposed rule to eat nothing except rotla[1], flat unleavened millet bread, and mung, a type of pulse. One day, someone ate his rotlas by mistake. He started a tantrum. The head cook offered to make him some fresh rotlas in an attempt to calm him down, but he was already huffing and puffing on his way straight to Swamiji. Swamiji was in his meeting room with some important delegates who had come to see him for the first time. In a burst of fury, the man stormed into the room and shouted, "Look at the head cook? I eat only mung and rotla and still he doesn't make them for me? They don't look after me..." Swamiji knew his temperament well, listened patiently to his fiery outburst. Swamiji apologized and excused himself from the meeting. To settle such a trivial problem, he called the

---

[1] A round roti cooked out of Bajra flour

head cook and politely requested him to make rotla and mung every day. The head cook stated the actual position, but Swamiji just repeated the same polite appeal. Later, around 12:30, Swamiji sat down for lunch. The person in question was sitting behind the sadhus, at the back of the room near the doorway. Swamiji caught a glimpse of him and lovingly called him near. Swamiji affectionately gave him some prasad of mung and rotla. No scolding. No punishment. Even though Swamiji had been placed in a very embarrassing situation, he did not reprimand the person for his disgraceful behavior the previous day. Overwhelmed by Swamiji's saintliness and selfless love, he broke into tears. In one sentence, Swamiji later described, "He came to me like a ravenous lion let loose from his cage" (Anandswaroopdas, 1998).

Apart from celibacy, free of avarice and ego-free, the other virtues are also necessary for a leader to serve better. Swamiji possessed virtues like simplicity, integrity, humility, forget & forgive, detachment to belongings and many others. I have mentioned just a few necessary ones from the life of Swamiji.

Simplicity

"In character, in manner, in style, in all things, the supreme excellence is simplicity."
~ Henry Wadsworth Longfellow ~

Swamiji had a base of a million followers close to him. Many of them possessed luxurious cars, chartered planes, and abundance of other luxuries. But Swamiji kept his simplicity intact. Once Swamiji was to meet a great religious world leader. On 6th April 1984, A reporter from Reuters News Mr. Phillip asked Swamiji, "What will you wear when you meet him?" Swamiji said, "We wear this same dress all year." The reporter said, "But he wears costlier dress and gold ornaments. Won't you feel inferior?" Swamiji said, "We follow our vows and let him follow his. It doesn't make any difference" (Kpdas, Pramukhcharitramrut Sagar Part 4, 2009). People change their dress as per the event, season, fashion & country. It was astonishing that he wore a pair of long saffron wardrobe style cloth his entire life. No change to it ever! He would wear it until it was too old and compelled to change. Once it was Diwali and an attendant sadhu requested him to wear a new pair. Many others insisted forcefully. To please them, Swamiji put on a new pair, but the next day, it was back to his old pair. Once he was on a visit, the upper garment was torn at its end. Despite using a new one, he stopped at weaver's shop and got it repaired (Kpdas, Pramukhcharitramrut Sagar Part 3, 2009). Once his attendant sadhu brought a silver spoon for his use. He refused to use it.

16th April 2005 in New York. Mr. K.C. Patel requested Swamiji, "In 2007, the BAPS is completing 100 years of its establishment. We propose to celebrate in your presence here in America. We intend to arrange for a helicopter for your convenience. Swamiji said, "What is the use of it? We are good with whatever is there." Devotees of America have repeatedly proposed a helicopter for Swamiji, but Swamiji never agreed for it (Vicharan Report April 2005).

Swamiji preferred economy class travel. In the early years, he used to travel by 3rd class in trains. His attendant sadhus said, "You are the president of an organization. We can afford it. Why don't you travel in 1st class?" Swamiji said, "It's Ok. We need to reach our destination. It's charity money; we should not use it for our comforts."

Once Swamiji's glasses were broken. A devotee said, "I will bring a new set of spectacles for you."

Swamiji commented, "Change the glasses only. The frame is intact." The devotee argued, "But it doesn't cost much for the frame. You have been using this old one for the last few years." Swamiji countered his argument, "Do I see through glasses or the frame? Please fit new glasses in the same frame" (Kpdas, Pramukhcharitramrut Sagar Part 3, 2009).

23rd May 2004, Edison. After prayers, Jaiminbhai was driving Swamiji to his home in a BMW. It was a comfortable ride. Jaiminbhai requested, 'Swamiji! If you agree, let me donate it while you travel in India. It will add comfort." Swamiji responded unattached, "No, I don't need it. Whatever is available there is fine." Jaiminbhai said, "This has been my wish for a long time, and it is convenient. If you accept, I will be pleased." Swamiji said, "Let things be as they are! We are all right." Others around also joined Jaiminbhai, but Swamiji didn't accept it (Vicharan Report May 2004).

Integrity

Northouse has summarized five central traits out of various trait researches. One of them is integrity. "Integrity is the quality of honesty and trustworthiness. People who adhere to a strong set of principles and take responsibilities for their actions are exhibiting integrity" (Northouse, Leadership: Theory and Practice, 2016, p. 25).

President Bill Clinton met Swamiji in 2000 in Miami and said, "I saw integrity in his eyes" (Pramukh Swami Maharaj blesses Bill Clinton at Akshardham, Gandhinagar, India, 2001). Swamiji inaugurated the Akshardham in Delhi on 6th November 2005. Devotees from different parts of India were scheduled to arrive there on that given date. Prior to that, a token fee of Rs. 100 was taken from each to confirm their arrival. After the celebration was over, Swamiji called the administrators and said, "Return the token money to all those who have not come here" (Kpdas, Pramukhcharitramrut Sagar Part 6, 2009). When there was an earthquake at Bhuj in January 2001, numerous organizations trusted BAPS for donations. Swamiji instructed the flood relief administration that every penny must be spent on flood relief only. "Whatever donation we receive for any project, it should be used for that only."

Some children brought flowers while Swamiji was offering prayers in Leicester. Swamiji called them and asked, "How do you arrange for these?" They said, "We pluck it from neighbor's gardens. We have got the permission for two roses, but we pluck three." Swamiji said, "It's not fair. Don't bring it from tomorrow. I don't need flowers during my prayers" (Jeva Me Nirkhya Re - 7, 1995, p. 71). Swamiji taught them the lessons of honesty for a lifetime.

Humility

"The best index to a person's character is how he treats people who can't do him any good."

~ Abigail Van Buren ~

On a festival day in Bochasan, 20 poor people from a lower cast arrived to meet Swamiji. It was 2.30 pm. They arrived outside Swamiji's room. Swamiji saw them and called them. They were overjoyed at this personal opportunity. They offered the garlands they had prepared with love and devotion. Swamiji accepted them and said, "You are poor so don't spend money on garlands or flowers. God will be pleased merely by your firm observance of moral rules" (Kpdas, Pramukhcharitramrut Sagar Part 6, 2009).

In 1995, Mahant Swami Maharaj through his experience opined, "Swamiji meets thousands of people; still, he doesn't neglect even the smallest child. His manners are modern, but his ideals are traditional – in harmony with the teachings of the ancient Vedas and other Hindu scriptures. His powers are infinite, yet his humility is second to none! So far apart are these extremes that he remains an enigma to thousands throughout the world – "Is such a man of flesh and blood possible in today's frenzied society?" (Kjdas, 1997).

Swamiji welcomed all with love and hospitality, regardless of their caste or status. He said, "People are no high or low for their castes. One who does good deeds is a true person; cast doesn't make any difference" (Pramukh Swami Maharaj - Life & Work in Brief, 2013, p. 99).

Despite his towering spiritual status, Swamiji never felt others be below him, useless, immoral or even ordinary. When he preached, he always adjusted according to people's moods and capacities. Despite being a leader of one of the largest organizations in the world, he had always mixed and mingled freely with others. He portrayed himself as a fellow traveler, walked alongside people instead of ahead (Viveksagardas, 1997).

After honoring Swamiji on 16th May 2004 at New York, the State Assemblyman of New York, David McDonna expressed his feelings and said: "I very much appreciate, and I am moved by what you do in this world, especially for the poor. And the feeling of the family you have promoted, that thought has touched me." Swamiji said, "There is no poor or rich in God's eyes. All are equal in the eyes of God. Whoever is in this world belongs to God only. If you work with such attitude then you will be able to treat rich or poor as same. We have to endeavor for everyone's virtues and happiness" (Vicharan Report May 2004).

Many years ago, when cast discrimination was intense, the low caste built an Ashram 'Parixit Majmudar' at Navsari. They were disappointed as no dignitary agreed to inaugurate it. To everyone's surprise, Swamiji went there and inaugurated it. There is a sacred holy place Zanzarka Tirth in Gujarat, India. It belonged to the subjugated cast. Atmarambhai invited Swamiji there. Swamiji went there. Due to years of discrimination, the people felt inferior to touch Swamiji. Swamiji called them nearer and hugged them. For the first time, they felt important. Swamiji spent time with them, de-addicted them from alcohol and other addictions, and inspired them to lead a noble and respectful life (Kpdas, Pramukhcharitramrut Sagar Part 6, 2009).

The Mayor of Nairobi Mr. Nathan Kaharra was very impressed with Swamiji's modest personality. That is why he sent his motorcar for Swamiji to visit Nairobi

City Council, and then return to the temple. Swamiji started a conversation with the driver using the interpreter, returning to the temple in the mayor's motorcar. He lovingly inquired details about his family life. The driver was surprised. How is this guest! How close he has come to my life in this short introduction! He was driving the Mayor and other dignitaries for many years. But who took such an interest in him? Who cared for him? He joyously asked, "Swamiji, do you have time? If you have time, I would drive you through this car and show you whole Nairobi" (Brahmopanishad, 1992, p. 84).

Major General Vikram Madan (Member, Dept. of the Australian Multicultural Commission) paid tribute, "Two days after the terrorist attack, Pramukh Swami Maharaj prayed for the peace of souls of not only 33 pilgrims and 3 Commandos, but also for the two terrorists' souls also. What else could be a greater and nobler example of forgiveness? What Pramukhwami Maharaj did was unimaginable. The tragic incident at Akshardham had developed such a belief that it is not necessary that every time a little spark sets Gujarat on fire. Swamiji's work was one of the best exemplary works of restraint and responsibility. I had the fortune to meet Pramukhswami Maharaj twice or more. At the end of those meetings, my heart experienced ultimate peace and happiness (Swaminarayan Bliss December 2016, p. 22).

Forget & Forgive

"Weak can never forgive. Forgiveness is the attribute of the strong."
~ Mahatma Gandhi ~

People suffer because they keep recalling their past over and over again. Those who can forget the past and forgive the culprits can focus and shape their future. When Nelson Mandela was released from jail, he said, "I am leaving the past here, if I bring it with me, I will be still in jail." Great leaders don't remember miseries. Swamiji once said, "We should keep & remember only positive accounts, and forget the negative forever."

The Biliya Satsang Mandal came for Swamiji's darshan. Years ago, when Swamiji visited Biliya, the entire village had some misconception about Swamiji. During the visit to the mandir, they insulted Swamiji. After some years they settled in the city of Surat. Their minds changed after they became aware of real facts. They came to Swamiji and urged, "It is unfortunate to remember that we insulted you in our village. We have to take you back to our village. We apologize and want to honor you at our village. We are here to invite you." Swamiji laughed and said, "Respect-insult does not affect me. I had to do the darshan of God. After darshan, the insult has been mitigated" (Vicharan Report May 2004).

Once, some opponents formed a plot to convict Swamiji. A Police Sub Inspector (PSI) was persuaded to arrest Swamiji. Swamiji was going to perform darshan at the same time the PSI was ordered the arrest. Swamiji stood calmly and patiently. The sadhus standing nearby asked for a warrant. There was no warrant. So, they called Gandhinagar for an investigation. There was no such order from there for Pramukh Swami Maharaj. They were exposed. The PSI was fearful and said, "What will happen now?" He trembled, but Swamiji called him lovingly. It was time to dine. Swamiji made him sit for the meal beside him. He fed him taking a special interest (Brahmopanishad, 1992, p. 94).

Detachment to Belongings

"Detachment is not that you should own nothing. But that nothing should own you." ~ Ali ibn abi Talib ~

Attachment to activity, things & people brings pain parallelly. Swamiji was associated with so many activities, but he was not attached emotionally to any of them. He could release himself at the next moment from any activity despite his involvement at its peak. The same was true for his belongings. He never felt something missing or lost.

12 January 2003 Swamiji was in Mumbai. There was a call from Dharmkuvar Swami, Bhadara. He informed Swamiji about the fire at Bhadara, and that all of Swamiji's belongings had been burnt. Swamiji said, "Good it is God's will. I am happy with the fact that no one is injured. Loss of material things is not worth worrying about" (Kpdas, Pramukhcharitramrut Sagar Part 3, 2009). Despite the news that his room was burnt down, Swamiji did not express any regret.

"Nearly all man can stand adversity, but if you want to test a man's character give him power."

~ Abraham Lincoln ~

9. Polite

"Politeness is to human nature what warmth is to wax."
~ Arthur Schopenhauer ~

The job of a leader is to get the best out of their team, community, country, etc. A true leader can win over people regardless of their nature through politeness. For a leader, Politeness is concerned with the importance of followers. The importance here is not how much rich or clever the individual is. It is about valuing an individual as a creation of God. Swami Vivekanand said, "Each soul is potentially divine." When we see everyone for their intrinsic value, not the skills or usefulness, it creates a positive environment and fosters healthy mutual relationships (Goleman, 2004). Politeness is to respect others and apologize for one's mistakes to others. One should also respect other's opinions and show humility towards them.

Respect for Others

"Politeness is nothing without respect."
~ Brandon Escriba ~

Philosopher Immanuel Kant (1724–1804) argued that it is our duty to treat others with respect. To do so means always to treat others as ends in themselves and never as means to ends. As Beauchamp and Bowie (1988, p. 37) pointed out, "Persons must be treated as having their own autonomously established goals and must never be treated purely as the means to another's personal goals." These writers then suggested that treating others as ends rather than as means requires that we treat other people's decisions and values with respect. Failing to do so would signify that we were treating them as a means to our own ends (Northouse, Leadership: Theory and Practice, 2016).

Leaders who respect others also allow them to be themselves, with creative wants and desires. They approach other people with a sense of their unconditional worth and valuable individual differences (Kitchener, 1984). Respect includes giving credence to others' ideas and confirming them as human beings.

Once a sadhu asked Swamiji, "Some people don't follow your instructions. Don't you get irritated by it?" Swamiji replied, "He will do it in the future. Getting irritated doesn't fulfill any means. I am happy with them also." He always said, "Politeness is more effective over power. We must respect others; even those who don't listen. Politeness always works. Everyone should master it. If the other person doesn't respect you, don't worry about it. You must respect them" (Kpdas, Pramukhcharitramrut Sagar Part 7, 2009).

In the book, 'Transformational Leadership' Joshua Medcalf says, "You matter. Not your achievements, what you do, your goals, your stuff, not your dreams. You matter" (Medcalf & Gilbert, 2017).

Pramukh Swami Maharaj valued everyone for first being a human being, and second, a valuable creation of God. While Delhi Akshardham was under construction, the artisans were carving the stones at Sikandara. Swamiji visited the site. Swamiji went to all the craftsmen and sprinkled flowers on the stone molds. Then he placed flowers on every artisan's head. He was offering his deep respect for their service and blessed them all.

Swamiji was tired due to delicate health and was 82 years of old age. Despite this, he was not bothered as he moved in two big sheds with zeal and was prepared to move to the third shed. In the third shed, he also blessed all the craftsmen and appreciated their art and encouraged them all (Vicharan Report 2003).

Sadhuvallabh Swami had noted at an event: "In 1985, Aksharbrahman Gunatitanand Swami's 2nd centenary birth anniversary program was organized in the village of Kurai in Vadodara district for Swamiji. After dinner, we all gathered outside our rooms. Swamiji asked Chhagan Bhagat of Thakaria (a low caste devotee) to sing a devotional song. He started singing and then remembered Yogiji Maharaj's events. Swamiji asked a sadhu to bring a camera. Swamiji stood as if he was with a king, with Chhagan who was leading a very ordinary life, and he continued to immortalize the image of Chhagan's worship. After that, when he arrived in Mumbai, he reminded me, "Have you sent the photograph to Chhagan?" (Jeva me Nirkhya re - 6, 1995, p. 119).

Apologize

Politeness is to apologize for one's mistake. Swamiji was a spiritual leader. He never felt embarrassed to apologize for a mistake regardless of him making it or not.

On 1st March 2001, Swamiji visited the village of Siddhpur. There was a planned visit to Shambhubhai Patel's house. It was the first home to be visited. Due to some communication confusion with the local volunteer's, Swamiji missed his home. Swamiji felt very sorry for it. When Shambhubhai came to meet him, Swamiji apologized and said, "We thought that the stay and meal were planned at your home, so we first reached the temple for darshan. Later we learned that the stay was arranged at the temple. We could not visit your home though it was on the way. Please forgive us" (Vicharan Report March 2001).

27th September 2003, Bhavnagar. Nitinbhai Palan and Markandbhai arrived from London to meet Swamiji at Bhavnagar. Swamiji had arranged for a car to receive them at the airport, but it arrived late, and they came in a hired car instead. Swamiji was disappointed and apologized to the devotees (Kpdas, Pramukhcharitramrut Sagar Part 3, 2009).

Swamiji had so much respect for his devotees, such that he could apologize even if he had not made a mistake. It was the last day of the 31-day Yogiji Maharaj Centenary and Gandhinagar Akshardham Inauguration celebrations in 1992. On the Swaminarayan Nagar festival site, there were 17,000 dedicated volunteers seated. Their months of selfless efforts had made the entire celebrations possible, and Swamiji wanted to express his heartfelt gratitude for their voluntary service. The assembly featured many emotional recollections of the celebrations, samuh arti, and pushpanjali. Finally, Swamiji rose to bless the volunteers, "You have all performed extraordinary service, which cannot even be described. Even if I perform hundreds of thousands of prostrations to you all, it would not be enough. Please forgive me if you have had to face any difficulties. You have all offered flowers to me, but I also want to offer flowers to you all."

With this, Swamiji took a big rose garland, and as he held it up to honor the volunteers, he became emotional. All the volunteers and sadhus seated, also overcome with emotion. There was silence. This respectful silence between guru Pramukh Swami Maharaj and his devotees left a lasting impression in the hearts of everyone present that day (Kpdas, Pramukhcharitramrut Sagar Part 4, 2009).

Swamiji never had a feeling of superiority over others. He never exploited his powers. He was always very polite while asking someone to carry out his duties. He valued other's rights and emotions.

Bhaktikishore Swami remembers an incident, "The passing away of Yogiji Maharaj on 23rd January 1971, had left the whole of Gujarat numb. A memorable incident unfolded during those difficult days. Swamiji had gone with the Trustees to Akshar Vadi to select the site for Yogiji Maharaj's last rites. The place where the current Yogi Smruti Mandir is was ultimately chosen. That's where I had planted some wheat. And it had grown rather well. On the morning of the 24th January 1971, at about 9 am, Swamiji called me & began softly, 'Bhakti, you know the Trustees, and senior devotees have chosen the cremation site. It's where you have grown the wheat. So, what shall we do now?"

The president of the organization was asking me, an ordinary, pure sadhu. It was like a king asking his servant. I was put to great embarrassment. "Swami,' I exclaimed meekly, "Whatever you've decided is fine. You don't have to ask me."

"You did plant the wheat yourself,' Swamiji explained politely. "You've worked hard for it, so of course we have to ask you." My insides churned seeing Swamiji so modest and caring (Divine Memories - 1, 1997, p. 59).

10. Fearless

"Let us not pray to be sheltered from dangers but to be fearless when facing them."
~ Rabindranath Tagore ~

A significant difference between leaders and non-leaders is how they cope with fear. Who wins? Fear or their mission? There was an incident with Martin Luther King, Jr. on 27th January 1956. Martin Luther King Jr. received a threatening phone call that night. The person on the other side snarled with hatred, "Listen, nigger, before next week you will be sorry you ever came to Montgomery." The phone call frightened him, and he worried about his wife and newborn baby. He could not sleep that night and in a moment of weakness thought of dropping out as a leader of the movement he was so passionate about. He prayed before God and apologized. He struggled with his emotions, and at last his inner voice won over his fear. After that, he once said, "If one day you find me sprawled out dead, I do not want you to retaliate with a single act of violence. I urge you to continue protesting with the same dignity and discipline you have shown so far" (George, Buhrman, & McLean, Martin Luther King Jr., A Young Minister Confronts the Challenges of Montgomery, 2007). If Martin Luther King had not conquered his fear, he could not lead. Gandhiji was a timid and fearful person until he started his advocate practice. But he overcame his fear, which allowed him to lead the movement of independence.

The leaders initially struggle alone. People comment their deeds as foolish, doubt their capability, their success, and discourage them. Facing family, social & political pressures, leaders keep moving ahead. It's challenging to surpass this stage. But those who surpass it become leaders. Pramukh Swami Maharaj faced a lot of threats and difficulties. People wrote against him in newspapers, insulted him in public places, but he was by nature, fearless. We can judge his fearless nature from some incidents.

Yagneshwar Swami describes an incident, "The 5th of June 1973, was a day I'll never forget. Through a jungle ride at 4:30 pm we left Untwada[2] for Junagadh. In our car, a Fargo, along with Bapa was Dr. Swami, Anupam Bhagat (presently Bhagwatpriya Swami), Devcharan Swami, Pragat Bhagat, A. R. Patel, two other devotees and myself. The route would take us through the Gir Jungle. Shortly after entering the jungle, we came to a junction by a small dam. None of us were sure which way to go, and so the driver, Damjibhai, stopped the car and asked Swamiji, 'Which road shall we take?'

"Take a left turn," replied Bapa. I don't know whether or not Damjibhai heard correctly, but he drove straight on. No one said anything. As we drove on into the night, we could see the jungle was becoming dense. Strangely, there wasn't a road sign, giving directions, anywhere. We were all becoming restless. It was now pitch dark outside, and we hadn't seen a car or any people for a long time. The road was becoming worse, and the fact that none of us knew where we were going was not comforting. But Damjibhai just drove on at full speed. Suddenly, someone shouted, 'Lion! Lion!'. We looked out of the window, and we could see a lion running alongside the car. After making sure all the windows were closed, Damjibhai slowed down the car so that we could have a proper look. A young, sturdy lion stood proudly in front of our car. Then it moved to the right and came and stood by Swamiji's door. There was silence, except for the sound of the frantic beating of our hearts. The lion stepped up and put its face to the window. We all held our breath. To our shock and horror, Swamiji rolled down his window! Then Swamiji and the lion just looked at each other. A whole minute must have elapsed, after which the lion simply turned around, and disappeared into the undergrowth!" When everyone else was frightened, the leader had a face-off with fear itself!

A leader is like a lion. A lion is the only animal who never steps back while it is being attacked. The lion tolerates the attack and still moves forward fearlessly — every other animal, even an elephant steps back, but not a lion. Swamiji was to build a mandir at Tithal. There was severe opposition, but Swamiji didn't step back. The devotees were threatened, sadhus were smashed, but he tolerated it all. There are many such stories of Swamiji keeping his stand on non-violence and moving ahead.

The root of fearlessness is faith in God. It was the guiding light of all the actions Gandhiji performed in any field. Faith did not sidetrack reason or contradict it. On the other hand, it transcended reason. Gandhiji had what he called a living faith in

---

[2] A small village

God, and he was sure of the existence of God more than he was of anything. The pursuit of truth was true bhakti or devotion to God. It was the path that led to God (Human Resource Management : A Gandhian Perspective, n.d.).

Once, some devotees booked Swamiji's tickets with Indian Airlines. Some days later, there were reports that terrorists had threatened to blast Indian Airlines flights. Everyone was now anxious about the journey and approached Swamiji to suggest to book with another airline. Swamiji said, "You trust the words of terrorists, and how is it that you don't trust God? Nothing will happen. We must fly by Indian Airlines." Finally, Swamiji flew on Indian Airlines and arrived fearlessly in London.

Faith in God as an all-doer release us from stress. For a leader, success is not guaranteed all the time, and failures are part of life. Faith in God enables him to accept the failures with ease. In June 2001, President APJ Abdul Kalam said, "Swamiji, when I first launched a rocket it failed, and I became very depressed and disheartened. At that time, I thought about becoming a sannyasi(monk), and give up everything." Swamiji replied, "We often say, 'Human effort and God's grace.' Even failure of the first rocket which you faced was for your good, and it prodded you to make things better. The way you have worked, for the invention of the rocket, brought success. God has ultimately given you success" (Fusion of Science and Spirituality, 2001). Swamiji was always stress-free anywhere, any time in any situation, for his faith in God, "God is all-doer."

On 4th July 2003 in Ahmedabad, Prof Mangalbhai Patel asked Swamiji, "How do you run 500 temples and so many social activities across the world so peacefully and stress-free?" Swamiji replied, "I don't run, God runs it all. We should put in an effort, pray to God, and leave the fruits up to God" (Vicharan Report July 2003). Swamiji advised that Faith in God as all doer, prayer and efforts are vital for success.

"If you can win over your mind, you can win over the whole world."

~ Sri Sri Ravi Shankar ~

11. Patience

"Patience is not simply the ability to wait - it's how we behave while we're waiting."
~ Joyce Meyer ~

A leader needs the patience to deal with people, to make effective decisions, to deal with the situations and difficulties. It requires patience to understand people and get comfortable to work with them effectively. A rash decision may cause considerable loss and regret later on. We can swim the ocean of difficulties through patience only. Patience and peace are very near to each other. Patience in problematic situations spreads the peace around.

Sunder Pichai had revealed his 'cockroach theory' for self-development. Here's how the theory goes: "At a restaurant, a cockroach flew and sat on a lady. She started screaming out of fear. Anyhow, she managed to push it away, but it landed on another person in the group, and the drama repeated. The waiter rushed to help them. Meanwhile, the cockroach next fell upon the waiter. The waiter was patient, he observed the cockroach on his shirt, waited for a little and then simply grabbed it and threw it out of the restaurant" (The 'Cockroach Theory' Of Sundar Pichai, n.d.). The incident inspired Sunder Pichai on how to tackle difficulties. The story is about patience. Look, wait and go!

Patience is the first step to handle any crisis. It's an outcome of wisdom. Here is an incident of how Swamiji kept his composure and dealt with a terrorist attack on Akshardham.

Pramukh Swami Maharaj gifted a gem called the 'Akshardham' to Gandhinagar, the capital of Gujarat, India. It took over 20 years to build. It is one of the most beautiful creations of Swamiji. People who visit Gujarat, most often visit

Akshardham. The whole monument is marvelously carved out of pink stone with no steel in its structure. This is a true masterpiece of ancient Indian temple building architecture. Large thematic gardens, astonishing surrounding corridors and a long pond with light-up fountains at the front multiply its elegance. In short, it's a wonderland for visitors.

For such a beautiful gem, it was a nightmare on the evening of 24th September 2002. A terrorist group targeted it for its popularity and crowd. Raju Thakur dropped two terrorists Mohammad Amjad (Lahore) and Hafiz Yaseen (Peshawar) aged 20 and 25 respectively from a white car at the Akshardham temple. They were armed with high-end automatic weapons and hand grenades. The terrorists climbed and jumped over the 7 feet periphery wall near gate no. 3 and began their rampage. They started firing their guns at 4.45 pm. Within a matter of minutes, they cruelly shot dead 33 people. One of the visitors, Sumitra was running away from the firing with a little boy and girl and was hit by a bullet on her leg. She pleaded with the terrorist, and with a nod from him, she watched in horror as he killed all three of them.

The perpetrators rushed towards the main shrine firing shots and throwing grenades at visitors around. Akshardham staff and temple supervisor Khodsinh Jadhav rushed across the 200-foot walkway and shut the 15-foot doors of the main shrine. The terrorist's motive to knock down the idol at the main shrine failed. Then, they tried to enter the exhibition halls full of visitors. Here, volunteers forcefully shut the exhibition center doors and saved more than 1000 lives. The terrorists then climbed to the top of hall number 3 and hid behind it after their heartless assassination act.

At 4.48 pm chief minister Narendra Modi was informed through an SOS call for help. Within 10-15 minutes, the state commando force and police covered the whole campus. Due to the 23 acres of large area, dense trees, and the evening approaching, it was difficult to locate the terrorists. They had the latest weapons compared to the local state commandos. The present force was not strong enough to combat the terrorists. At 5.15 pm, the Chief Minister of Gujarat requested help from the national security forces and two buses of deadly NSG (National Security Guards – Black Cat Commandos) arrived at Akshardham at 10.10 pm from New Delhi to execute "Operation Thunderbolt'. For the rest of the night, the troops continued firing at regular intervals in an attempt to locate the terrorists. The terrorists responded with intense firing and kept moving to different locations.

The search for the terrorists continued throughout the night. At around midnight, the terrorists jumped down from the parikrama and entered a nearby bathroom. The National Security Guards planned to pass the night until daybreak before attempting to locate the terrorists. During this time, the guards fired to draw fire from the terrorists, and consequently use up their ammunition. As the night progressed, the terrorists moved into another area, a grove of trees near exhibition hall 3. By daybreak, the terrorists became desperate, and the firing continued.

At approximately 6:45 am, the 14-hour-long ordeal ended with the Black Cat Commandos shooting the two terrorists hiding in the bushes. During this overnight search for the attackers, one state police officer and one commando lost their lives. Another commando, Surjan Singh Bhandari, was seriously injured and died in May 2004, after being comatose for two years. Akshardham volunteers Mahendrabhai M. Patel aged 33, Bachubhai C. Jadav (34), Kiranbhai B. Mali (27) and Bhaveshbhai M. Zala (19) sacrificed their lives resisting the assassinators. NSG commando Sureshkumar Yadav, SRP commando Arjunsinh (28) and A.H. Umedkar (23) also lost their lives combating terrorists. There was a total of 33 fatalities.

BAPS president Pramukh Swamiji was 125 km away at Sarangpur. P. Yogicharan Swami reported the casualty numbers to Pramukh Swamiji. Swamiji was counseling some visitors regarding their problems. He heard the news and continued with those visitors. The visitors were stunned to hear the news. But they were very grateful to Swamiji for giving them enough time to solve their problems at such a critical time. They felt Swamiji was far more concerned about them than what had happened. Once, the session was over with them, Swamiji then focused on the attack news.

At first, he prayed for a few minutes and then took a few quick decisions. Swamiji immediately sent some sadhus to Akshardham. He also decided to appeal for peace through the media to avoid any consequences of violence or riots. The peace note to the press officials was as follows:

"Though it is a sad incident, anyone may get disturbed and lose patience. At this miserable occasion, we need to control our emotions and maintain peace. Everyone should pray for harmony and peace. At such a critical moment we should seek solace in each other. We must unite to face the situation. I pray that in future a thing like this should not repeat, anywhere. I am grateful to those who have shown their sympathy to us. I offer my tribute to all those who have lost their lives."

There were a series of consolation phone calls from political authorities, various social organizations and well-wishers. Swamiji took a firm non-violence stand and inspired everyone for peace. It was Swamiji's incredible influence over his one million followers and the general public. No one got aggressive. All of them respected Swamiji's peace appeal. There was not a single incidence of violence throughout the country. Everyone admired Swamiji's leadership qualities (Vicharan Report September 2002).

Mumford and colleagues defined one of the social judgment skills as 'Social Performance.' It means leaders need to be able to communicate their vision to others. Skill in conflict resolution is an essential aspect of social performance competency (Northouse, Leadership: Theory and Practice, 2016, p. 50). Swamiji could communicate his peace appeal very effectively to his one million close followers and the 1.2 billion citizens of India. It was conflict resolution through a peace appeal.

Numerous other leadership qualities came to be validated and proven with Swamiji in this situation. In the 1990s leadership researchers like Goleman, Wolfe, Mayer, Salovey & Caruso coined the concept of Emotional Intelligence. They explored it as a leader's ability to understand and reason with emotions, and to effectively manage emotions within oneself and in relationships with others. Goleman extended the concept to social competence to consist of empathy and social skills such as communication and conflict management (Goleman, 2004). The Akshardham attack could have led to long-term communal conflicts, but Swamiji successfully managed it. He could communicate his vision of non-violence to followers and the entire nation very effectively, and that too, promptly. He could control his emotions as well as that of others.

It's a surprise that he was so stable at that time. After he sent some sadhus to Akshardham to handle the crisis, a few minutes later he continued with his scheduled meetings to build a student's hostel and a state-of-art hospital in Surat. At one end, terrorists were busy killing, and on the other end, Swamiji was busy planning a state-of-art hospital for patients. Chief Minister Narendra Modi called Swamiji for consolation. He was shy and hesitated to talk. Swamiji broke the silence and solaced him, "Don't worry, take care of your health. Everything will settle." Narendrabhai recalled this moment on 7th December 2002, in Gandhinagar. He said, "Pramukh Swamiji is an awesome leader. I can't forget the moment I called Swamiji immediately after the attack. He was stable, comfortable and stress-free. I called to offer my consolation, but instead, he solaced and motivated me with his kind words. He didn't ask me a single question about what would happen to Akshardham? Swamiji's self-control and stability were amazing. It was his influence on people that allowed them to peacefully tolerate the attack" (Vicharan Report December 2002).

Zaccaro (2002), a well-known researcher on Leadership Trait Theory had illustrated Social Intelligence as the ability to select and enact the best response given the contingencies of the situation and social environment (Northouse, Leadership: Theory and Practice, 2016). Swamiji's response, in this case, proved his social intelligence. Marlowe (1986), had emphasized on understanding one's own and others' feelings, and act appropriately. Swamiji received news from Akshardham that several hundred visitors were stuck at the exhibition halls and would not be let out until the terrorists were caught. Swamiji instructed Vishwavihari Swamiji to make arrangements for water, food and washroom facilities for them (Vicharan Report September 2002).

At 12.35 pm, volunteers informed Swamiji that a monk Parmeshwar Swami was shot dead. Swamiji told them to keep it quiet, because if it was reported in the news; it could ignite public excitement. Their sentiments towards the monk could result in communal riots.

After intensive research Zacarro, Kemp and Bader had enlisted Emotional Stability, Emotional Intellect and Problem Solving as great leader's trait. We saw all these qualities in Swamiji at this crucial event.

Stodgill (1974) had talked about the leader to be successful in different situations. He characterized tolerance, persistence, and influence as necessary traits for a leader. Swamiji proved these qualities as well.

The next morning security guards arrived at Sarangpur to protect Swamiji against any suspected danger. Swamiji was on his routine walk outside his residence. The security guards created a parameter so that everyone had to stay at a several feet distance. Swamiji didn't like it. He overrode the security and continued meeting his visitors and called for the Sadhus to remain near him, like always. He prioritized social relationships over his safety. There was a grand festival 'Shraddha-Parva' and tons of milk-pudding was prepared. Swamiji canceled the celebration and distributed the milk-pudding to amongst the villagers instead.

On 29th September 2002, at 11 am Swamiji arrived at the Civil Hospital in Ahmedabad. He said, "Please do not hurry, I want to meet and talk to each victim at length." He met the wounded volunteers & commandos, inquired and listened to them. Everyone was grateful to see a great leader by their bedside. Then, Swamiji went to Akshardham and walked through the passage where pilgrims had been shot dead. He prayed for their salvation and sprinkled flowers there. Next, he arrived at the location where the terrorists were shot dead. With the same devotion, Swamiji prayed for them and sprinkled flowers there too. Swamiji's forgiveness and mercy touched everyone deep in their heart.

Crisis, pressure, social beliefs, and trends could not influence Swamiji. They could not deviate Swamiji from his goal of spreading peace and serving people at his best for the common good. He was residing on a platform above all external differences where he could see everyone as divine and just human beings.

BAPS also organized a condolence meeting after the attack. The prayer assembly commenced with devotional prayers sung by sadhus for the peace of the departed souls, grieving relatives, and all sympathizers. Then, the entire gathering observed a 2-minute silent prayer for the deceased, injured, and killed.

Mumford, Zaccaro, Hardin (2000) developed the Skills Approach leadership model. It consists of three competencies: Problem Solving, Social judgment skills, and Knowledge. The problem-solving skills are a leader's creative ability to solve new and unusual, ill-defined organizational problems. Leader formulates new understandings about the problem and generates prototype plans for problem solutions. Being able to construct solutions plays a unique role in problem-solving (Northouse, Leadership: Theory and Practice, 2016, p. 48).

Akshardham Response

Swamiji's unique response to modern terrorism was coined as 'Akshardham Response.' The Akshardham attack and the response to it became a case study for the NSG (National Security Guard). Brigadier Raj Seetapathy, the NSG commando in-charge of the rescue mission called 'Operation Thunderbolt' or 'Operation Vajra Shakti,' asserted that the response to Akshardham terror attack had become a benchmark of clock-work achievement. The brigadier presented this case study, Akshardham Response: How to challenge an attack with calm and peace, at various centers, including the Sardar Patel Police Academy in Hyderabad and various Army training sessions. The Brigadier said, "What Pramukh Swami Maharaj did was unbelievable. He pieced society back together. The Akshardham tragedy instilled a sense of confidence that Gujarat need not burn at every spark that is ignited. What I observed after the operation was the calm and serenity that was quickly restored. I have faced many violent encounters in my professional life, but the Akshardham response was great learning both from an operational and philosophical point of views." The brigadier said that once the spiritual head decided to purify the souls of the two terrorists, the volunteers and devotees immediately fell silent. "There was no slogan shouting, no anger being expressed for any community. It was one of the most noble and exemplary acts of restraint and responsibility that foiled the design of terrorists to spark more violence" (Akshardham Temple Attack, n.d.).

Outcomes of Patience

Leadership Outcomes are measured on two points in skills leadership model: Problem Solving and Performance. The criteria for good problem solving are determined by the originality and the quality of expressed solutions to problems. Excellent problem solving involves creating solutions that are logical, effective and unique. Go beyond given information. (Zaccaro et al., 2000).

Performance: Performance outcomes reflect how well the leader has done her on his job. To measure performance standard external criteria is used. If the leader has done well and been successful, the leader's evaluations will be positive. The Akshardham response was first of its kind against the terrorism, ever. The most significant outcome: There was not a single negative consequence of this catastrophe.

If we look at the following reviews and comments on the Akshardham attack and what people had to say about Swamiji, we are convinced that Swamiji has provided us a new, effective, successful solution which performed very well at such a delicate time when terrorism is on the radar of every nation.

"There is no known example of such a great mercy and forgiveness." – Major Vikram Madan (Member, South Australian Multicultural Commission) (Swaminarayan Bliss December 2016, p. 22).

"Srimad Bhagwatam highlights six virtues of a saint. Tolerance, Patience, Compassion, Forgiveness, Friendliness to enemies and devotion. I saw all these at its peak in Pramukh Swamiji." – Shrutidharmdas, Iskon Temple (Swaminarayan Bliss December 2016, p. 10).

"I have been much associated with terrorism cases. As a secretary to the home ministry, this is my regular job. I learned the lesson of peace from Swamiji. It was the greatest gift & lesson to mankind." – Michael Balboni (Senator, New York) (Vicharan Report April 2004).

"I congratulate you because no procession took place. Aggressive organizations could not deviate you from your own identity." – Veer Sanghavi (Hindustan Spokesman, Kolkata) (Vicharan Report September 2002).

"I heard Gandhiji's soul in the voice of Swamiji's. In his blessings at tribute assembly, he didn't utter the word 'terrorism or terrorists.' Gujarat survived his pious decision otherwise riots might claim ten thousand innocent lives. It really saved the country from communal conflicts." – B. Swaroop

"Pramukh Swamiji is a holy man who teaches love and character." – Frank Plove Jr., Edison, 05-06-2004 (Vicharan Report June 2004).

"Swamiji is just a 6th standard pass fellow. I can't understand how he can lead such a noble movement. At the Akshardham attack, he didn't get angry. If would have casually said, 'Whatever happened is not fair.' It might put entire Gujarat state and Country on fire. I can feel his influence on people at large" (23-06-2005, Rajkot) – Mr. Tushar (Director, All India Radio Station) (Vicharan Report June 2005)

"Swamiji spread the faith, tolerance, generosity, and high moral values. I believe that the world needs such a leader. There are challenges of terrorism. We need Swamiji to spread wisdom, non-violence, and compassion among religious groups" – Robert Black (Deputy Chief of Mission) 9-7-2005, New Delhi (Vicharan Report July 2005).

"The world felt the power of peace over terror." – Arun Gujarati (Speaker, Senate) (19-10-07, Mumbai (Vicharan Report October 2007).

"Swamiji's empathy for those who attacked his best creation was matchless. He was so calm & stable on this disaster; it shows his heights of wisdom." – Ashok Bhatt (A prominent BJP leader) 22-03-2008, Sarangpur (Vicharan Report March 2008).

"I am connected to 100 management gurus. We manage through brain and Swamiji through the heart. I invite Swamiji and his team to teach us management." – Mr. Deepak Dalal (President, AEC, Gujarat)

"At the Akshardham event, Swamiji's peace appeal had a charismatic impact on society." -Bob Kaplan (Solicitor, Canada) 17-02-2011, Baroda (Vicharan Report February 2011).

"Pramukh Swami Maharaj is the most courageous man in the world. He dared build another Akshardham at New Delhi after the attack at Gandhinagar." – Kartikeyan (Major General, Indian Army) 18-11-2005, New Delhi (Vicharan Report November 2005).

"His single word could cost thousands of innocent lives and disrupt. May all leaders follow the path shown by Swamiji to maintain the world peace." – Gunavant Shah (A renowned writer) 10-11-05, New Delhi (Vicharan Report November 2005).

According to Mumford's Skills Leadership model, knowledge has a positive impact on how leaders engage in problem-solving. It is knowledge and expertise that make it possible for people to think about complex system issues and identify strategies for appropriate change. Furthermore, this capacity allows people to use prior cases and incidents to plan for needed change. It is the knowledge that allows people to use the past to constructively confront the future (Northouse, Leadership: Theory and Practice, 2016, p. 50).

Swamiji knew the past consequences of terrorist attacks at Godhra. He knew that revenge would take other thousands of innocent lives. Martin Luther King, Jr. said, "Darkness cannot drive out darkness, only light can do that. Hate cannot drive out hate; only love can do that." It was Swamiji's love that drove out hatred and flourished peace.

Happy Consequences

The Akshardham attack was a national crisis. The attack on a Hindu temple was planned to trigger communal riots in the nation. The prime minister Atal Bihari Vajpayeeji was on a trip to the Maldives. He returned immediately, and rushed to Akshardham, Gandhinagar. He said, "What has happened in Gujarat has horrified me. I was pained to see the developments on TV. Shamefully a holy shrine is used for such a dastardly act." The deputy prime minister Shri Lal Krishna Advaniji also rushed to the site (PM calls temple attack well-planned conspiracy, 2002).

Swamiji's non-violence stand earned magical happy returns. The attack was to disrupt the peace and harmony, but both improved due to Swamiji's response. The Muslim community was grateful to Swamiji for saving their lives. The next day after the attack, a group of Muslims from Botad visited Swamiji and apologized for the disaster. Swamiji told them to forget it and live peacefully. Another group of Muslim leaders arrived from Ahmedabad. They were surprised how Swamiji could control his emotions and didn't utter a single negative word about the assassination or anyone else? Ahmedbhai said, "It happened for the first time that Muslim leaders had condemned this event collectively. Swamiji, we are very much hurt that people from our community are involved in it. We apologize for that. We hope it doesn't happen again." Swamiji advised them to continue the brotherhood spirit and participate in the happy and sad events of other communities to boost peace and harmony." One of the leaders said, "In the Quran, it is said that one should be loyal to the country where he lives." Swamiji said, "I always tell our followers the same; to obey the laws of the country they live in and cooperate & help the local community" (Vicharan Report September 2002).

Brigadier Sitapathi was so touched by Swamiji's humility that after his retirement, he dedicated the rest of his life as a volunteer at Akshardham, New Delhi. He is now in charge of the security squad at Akshardham.

Mahant Swami Maharaj often points to a formula to solve problems. He says, "Don't go on Who is Right, take your decision taking into account What is Right? Who is right will lead to more complications and what is right will lead to a solution and peace." It requires patience to look into the matter to find out what is right? Through his wisdom and patience, Swamiji took a firm stand on what is right!

There is a difference between pleasure and peace. Peace stands high over pleasure. Swamiji knew the need of peace over pleasure. Revenge could earn emotional pleasure, but peace was more important and fruitful. Swamiji identified this basic need of peace; everyone has a deep thirst for it, and he fulfilled it through his pious decisions.

"Patience is bitter, but its fruit is sweet."
~ Jean Jacques Rousseau ~

12. Encouraging/Motivating

"Believe you can, and you are halfway there."
~ Theodore Roosevelt ~

A leader's job is to remove the dirt on a gem and shine it back to its beauty. The team may be discouraged due to failures, insufficient resources or other factors. The leader should be able to keep them motivated under any circumstance. A leader constantly motivates and encourages the followers towards the goal.

The Gunatitanand Swami Bicentennial Celebrations were going on in Ahmedabad. It was 2nd November 1985, and still, there were 40 days of the festival left. Sadhus and devotees were doing their best. There was a welcome ceremony for some dignitaries on stage.

Shrutiprakash Swami went to Swamiji and reported, "I'm leaving for Mumbai."

Swamiji: "Why? The festival is still going on."

"Yes, but my major department duties have been completed. I'm rather tired. I'll be back in a couple of days after some rest."

Swamiji didn't like what he had just heard.

Slowly Swamiji began, "You're still young, and you're already tired? We've come to serve here, you know! How can you think of anything else as long as our hands and feet are working?"

The conversation continued on stage. The dignitaries had been kept waiting. There was a long queue to attend to as well before Swamiji could get to the assembly on time. And here Swamiji was, talking to him. The others signaled to Swamiji to cut it short. Swamiji ignored them and continued, "Do as much as you can. But remember; it's no job, it's the service to the Lord."

This is a trait of a leader who encourages and reminds their followers what their purpose is. Swamiji's mere presence could inspire and encourage people. On 9th November 2004 in Delhi, someone asked a sadhu who was associated with the construction of Delhi Akshardham, "See, Swamiji arrived here today. According to you, what difference did it make?" The sadhu replied, "Before Swamiji arrived here, it was a routine job for the laborers and artisans. After we received news of Swamiji's arrival, Ishwarcharan Swamiji said to the labor and artisans, "Pramukh Swamiji is arriving, and he will see your work." It charged everyone with electrifying energy and their output doubled. They were encouraged to finish it as soon as possible" (Vicharan Report November 2004).

On 16th May 2008 in Sarangpur, BAPS led schools reported their overall standard 12 results to Swamiji. All schools received a 100% passing result, but one of the schools didn't get the desired result. One of the administrators was depressed with the results. Previously, he was very enthusiastic to report the results, but this time he hesitated. Swamiji brought him closer and asked, "How many failed this year?" He replied, "Seven." Swamiji said, "There is nothing to worry. You tried your best, though the results are not up to mark. Next year you may put more effort, and things will be settled" (Vicharan Report May 2008). The administrator's strength and energy was restored with these words.

"Patience is the companion of wisdom."

~ Saint Augustine ~

13: Problem Solving / Conflict Management

"Every problem has a solution. You just have to be creative enough to find it."
~ Travis Kalanick ~

A leader's essential responsibility is to solve organizational problems and human conflicts. The more a leader is good at it, the more he is successful at it. Leaders must have the ability to handle problems and seek acceptable and reliable solutions.

Pramukh Swami Maharaj was great at problem-solving and conflict management. If we look at it from a world perspective, it was a special mobile court! One wouldn't find a courtroom with any wooden benches, witness box, the judges, loudly arguing advocates. Instead, one would find a simple sofa and a rostrum, happy and peaceful argument free environment, a long queue of complainers waiting for their turn and Swamiji counseling with his smile and pious face solving each case very comfortably. People waiting in the queue would report their problem in minutes, and sometimes in seconds. All it took Swamiji was to respond to them in a concise period. One could find 700 to 1000 cases solved in a day: no holiday, no Sunday. Swamiji's spiritual court was active 365 days. Yes, when everyone finished, they were blessed with a box of sweets as well! No demand for any fees before, at that moment or after that. Everyone felt as if they were on the lap of their father or mother as they sought guidance from Swamiji. Let us term it as blissful abode instead of a court.

A Man of Decision

BAPS Ex-Secretary Harishbhai Dave an advocate by profession was heading the accounts and legal department of BAPS for more than 30 years. He shared his experiences with Swamiji as follows:

There was an institution which had numerous issues with BAPS - which needed to be settled. Everybody had tried but was unsuccessful. They were not willing to agree and always forwarded one reason or another for not agreeing. Every time they came up with new arguments. Problems lingered on for a long time. "Bapa, can you help?" asked Harisbhai. A meeting was called for. The representatives of that institution started with long arguments produced old files and made out a big case. Bapa listened patiently. He then explained the entire matter in a new perspective and its impact on public life. He quoted from past references and instances — no reference to any note or file. They were all amazed. Such a powerful memory. Such lucid explanation of events! A practical approach! Within moments the issues were resolved. The trustees of the institution agreed to BAPS' proposal. Everybody departed with a smile on their face (Shelat, 2017).

After the meeting, everyone went their way. There were some critical policy decisions left on behalf of the organization. Swamiji stopped us going, and within five minutes he made many extraordinary decisions. As an advocate, I was amazed at his capability. Once he gave 56 decisions in just 80 minutes. I can't forget his problem solving and decision-making skills ever (Mr. Harish Dave, Secretary BAPS) (Sadhu V., 1992, p. 303).

The CEOs or ministers or high officials keep personal assistants to help them, who give them advice whenever they needed it. Swamiji was different. He had everything figured out. He knew what, when, and why. He could coordinate everything like a supercomputer in his mind without notes or a diary. When the time demanded, he could reveal the very decision and particular details (Brahmopanishad, 1992).

Kirkpatrick and Locke postulated that leaders differ from non-leaders on six traits: drive, motivation, integrity, confidence, cognitive ability, and task knowledge (Northouse, Leadership: Theory and Practice, 2016).

Swamiji's conceivability to understand the question was equally remarkable. Once, there was an urgency for an important decision. Swamiji was in London. His physical presence was essential to understand the complications going through a map. We tried it over the phone. There was a dilemma in our mind. Without understanding the map, how would Swamiji understand it? Before we began explaining, Swamiji started giving feedback and provided his guidance.

Swamiji's cognitive abilities were matchless. He could recognize the person within seconds. He could X-ray his thoughts and mind. Swamiji could understand within a few seconds if the person was excited or confused, happy or anxious. It happened to us a few times that we had gone prepared with something and he would be able to pinpoint the areas we had forgotten to highlight. This made us more aware of being very particular and detail-oriented before we approached him because he was just so sharp. He could remember every past detail, and this meant that if he was discussing something, we had to go back and research the old files as his memory was equally compelling.

It was my first case at the supreme court. I was new there. My senior advocates told me that your case is technically weak, and we are sure you will lose. There is no chance in your favor. Swamiji gave me his blessing and guidance. I followed it, and I was able to defeat the opponents within a few minutes, and the decision was in our favor. Swamiji's understanding & knowledge of legal matters were always surprising to me (Brahmopanishad, 1992).

He had a vast knowledge of all the government administrative posts, their powers, and duties. Thus, when a situation arose, he was able to guide us as to whom we should meet. Through his powerful insight and knowledge, he never degraded us. He was so humble, we never felt his power nor were we ever afraid of him. For every discussion, he was involved, then able to detach himself and then move on to the next topic of discussion with the same level of attention and zeal.

Human Conflicts & Solutions

A manager can deal with task-related problems. A leader can resolve human conflicts. If one can settle human conflicts, other problems don't arise at all. Swamiji could understand human nature very well. He had mastered how to extinguish human conflicts and inspire them to work together forgetting and forgiving old matters.

There are two villages, Kukad, and Odarka in the Bhavnagar district, Gujarat, India. For the last 200 years, the Rajput citizens of both villages were hostile to each other and fought bitterly over a piece of disputed land. Many lost their lives due to this conflict. The volcano of hatred was so intense that the villagers had abstained from drinking water from each other's village. The hatred just grew. Through the decades, many arbitrators, like the Maharaja of Bhavnagar Krishnakumarsinhji, and British and Indian government officials had tried to resolve the conflict, but they failed.

But the deadlocked situation took a new turn with the transformation of Ramsangh Bapu. He was a hard-core criminal who wreaked terror in the region of Ghogha near Bhavnagar. He came into contact with Swamiji. Being a resident of Odarka, he expressed his remorse for his sins. He appealed to Swamiji to help resolve the hostility between Odarka and Kukad.

On 12th April 1990, Swamiji visited Odarka and went to the disputed land on the outskirts. Prayers were offered for the redemption of all those who had died in the conflict and for an end to the pledge of not drinking water from each other's village. The occasion climaxed when the Darbars drank water from each other's village offered by Swamiji. Swamiji dissolved two hundred years of vendetta in minutes. This historic event of extinguishing the fires of hatred and inspiring springs of love and friendship will forever be etched in the annals of history. Swamiji was extremely happy for the restoration of peace in the hearts of the people of Odarka and Kukad (Anandswaroopdas, 1998).

Burns's (1978) perspective argues that it is vital for leaders to engage themselves with followers and help them in their personal struggles regarding conflicting values. The resulting connection raises the level of morality in both the leader and the follower (Northouse, Leadership: Theory and Practice, 2016, p. 33).

On the 23rd April 2010 in Ahmedabad, Brahmvihari Swami describes Swamiji's love and compassion for solving personal problems. He recalled an incident, "That night I had to leave for a Satsang tour abroad. So, at 6.30 p.m. I went to Swamishri's living quarters to take his leave. I was amazed to see Swamiji absorbed in reading a letter. I went nearer to Swamiji and could not resist saying, "Bapa! You have a constant pile of letters to read. Don't you ever get tired!"

Swamiji didn't say anything and continued reading.

I repeated, "Swamiji! You read so many letters which, I think, are more than any government officer would read." Before I could say anything further, Swamiji looked at me and said, 'These are not the letters from an office. These are letters of love from the devotees. Reading them is not work, it is seva." In Swamiji's mind, reading letters and solving the problems of devotees tantamount to service and devotion. They were not a burden to him (Vicharan Report April 2010).

Swamiji has read and replied to letters in a variety of situations: during Satsang assembly, while traveling by car or train, on a railway platform, before his afternoon sleep, in an elevator, during a procession, and while talking on the phone. He attends to them whenever and wherever he is.

On the 14th of August 2005, there was a phone call from South India. The person was confused as to which floor he should buy his flat on. Swamiji said, "You may buy as per your requirement and to your favor." The man continued, "The building I have decided on has 12 floors, please guide me which floor I buy the flat on?" After some thought, Swamiji said, "You may buy on either the fourth, fifth or sixth floor." The man replied, "I will buy after you fix the floor." At last Swamiji replied, "Ok, I think the 3rd floor will be good" (Kpdas, Pramukhcharitramrut Sagar Part 5, 2009).

Divorce

Divorce is a modern burning problem. It is at its peak compared to just a decade or two ago. It not only separates a couple, but it leaves behind an uncertain future for their children and court cases for property issues. Swamiji helped solve this issue and saved many families and relations.

Swamiji learned about the divorce plan of a young devotee. Swamiji wished them to arrive at a compromise and said, "It's not only the fault of a single side. Both may have some fault. One should tolerate and accept both pleasure and pain. The guy should imagine what if this situation happened to his sister. The mother-in-law should treat her as a daughter." In London, Swamiji instructed the youths, "All of you should keep in mind that once you marry, never separate. You should be together till your last breath" (Brahmopanishad, 1992).

On 16th January 2006 in Mumbai, a youngster visited Swamiji. His wife left him after a dispute and wrote a 16-page letter to Swamiji explaining the problems. Swamiji told the young man, "This is not the way you behave in your family life. You should understand and fulfill your responsibilities at par. It took me an hour to read the entire letter. Live peacefully" (Kpdas, Pramukhcharitramrut Sagar Part 12, 2009).

Depression/Suicide

On 23rd April 2005 in Ahmedabad, three brothers came to see Swamiji. The elder brother lost his business, and the debt was so high, it was impossible to pay it back. Due to immense stress, he tried to commit suicide but survived, and a volunteer brought him to Swamiji. After listening to what happened Swamiji said, 'There are many people in the world who have debt, suicide is not a solution. Even if one loses billions of rupees, there is hope. Many people I know have overcome the situation. You have not made any mischief; your intention is to return the money. You must refund 100% of the money. Just go and with folded hands tell the creditor you will return the money, it will take time, but you will return it. If you are alive, you can pay it back with your efforts and earnings. Think, what will happen to your family?

Suicide is not a solution" (Vicharan Report April 2005). Swamiji prayed for him and blessed him. He got up and promised not to attempt suicide again.

An old man came to meet Swamiji with his son-in-law. He said, "My son constantly thinks of suicide. We have every luxury, but he is restless. He is angry all the time and scolds everyone around him." Swamiji said to him, "Don't sit idle. You are healthy, why think of suicide? Instead, start thinking about occupation and earning. Keep yourself busy with activities." Swamiji understood that due to idleness, his mind had become the devil's workshop.

On 14th September 2008 in Ahmedabad, a medical student was studying surgery, but he could not cope with his studies and became depressed. He said, "I think of suicide because I find it very hard. Though I work hard, I do not see the results. My seniors' torture me. I am scared. I can't pass the exams." Swamiji responded "If you think so, then change your stream and enroll for an easier course. Never think of suicide. Don't start any drugs as well. I will pray for you" (Vicharan Report September 2008).

Fear / Death

A little boy came to Swamiji and complained that he was scared of death. He was crying for two days. Swamiji was surprised how a child so young could be depressed about death to this extent. Then suggested to him, "Don't be scared. Do prayers and engage yourself with your studies." The child was charged up and moved on happily (Kpdas, Pramukhcharitramrut Sagar Part 12, 2009).

29th June 2007, Houston. Mr. Monzur Hourani originally from Lebanon was invited as Chief Guest for a meeting. He is a celebrated engineer and architect and member of many international institutes in the field. He came to Swamiji before the meeting. He said, "Despite all the success in life, I always feel something is missing. I am disturbed within. During the 1975 Lebanon war, I lost my mother and brothers. When I remember this, I get disturbed. I have only one question for God, why is he doing this?

Swamiji consoled him saying, "God doesn't discriminate, he does good to all. But it is human attitude, his nature, and ego that inflicts sorrow and pain, but we have to believe God, whatever he does is for good. Everyone has to die one day, How? That is uncertain. It is natural you get emotional remembering your dear ones. With advancement in technology, people will live longer, suffer less, but death is sure. So, to avoid sorrow, we need to cultivate personal wisdom. Mr. Monzur Hourani said, "I will continue with pious deeds and spend my wealth for charity." Swamiji said, "Pious deeds will bring you peace. Anything invested well never goes in vain. Keep faith in God, and you will be at peace" (Kpdas, Pramukhcharitramrut Sagar Part 12, 2009). Swamiji soothed a broken heart by counseling him and touched on the importance of wisdom and doing well for others.

Family Conflicts

There was a quarrel between the two groups of a village in Tajpur. They visited Swamiji on 25th June 1985 at Sarangpur. To both the groups, Swamiji advised, "We are one family. Tajpur is like our home. Now if you quarrel at home, then how we can talk about unity to the outside world? My humble request is that I have treated you all as relatives. All of you are present in my heart, never to leave it. There is no discrimination among sadhus. We are more satisfied with your prosperity and peace" (Pramukh Charitam).

In May 1988, Swamiji was on religious tour to London. One of the devotees filed a case in court against his son regarding a property dispute. Swamiji called him and said, "Why did you go to court? I am present. You should have reported it to me before you went to court. Remember! You will lose your money and peace of mind there. We are one family; I will meet your son and your advocates as well and make them understand. Then, Swamiji called his son and other relevant people and solved the matter within a few hours. Father and son both united as before, and the property problem solved. Everyone was happy with the solution. Swamiji said, "GOD and saint are our true friends, so seek their guidance in miseries of life" (Jeva me Nirkhya re - 6, 1995, p. 113).

"A good, patient ear is required to resolve conflicts."

~ Anonymous ~

13. Familyhood Traits

"To us, family means putting your arms around each other and being there."
~ Barbara Bush ~

*L*eadership or management books emphasizes human relationships. The Psychodynamic Approach under leader-follower relationships highlights that people often assume at an unconscious level, that the leader or organization can and should offer protection and guidance similar to that offered by parents. Groups subject to the dependency assumption are united by feelings of helplessness, inadequacy, neediness, and fear of the outside world (Northouse, Leadership: Theory and Practice, 2016).

In Skills Approach, Robert Katz had talked about human skills. He said, "These are 'people skills.' They are the abilities that help a leader to work effectively with followers, peers, and superiors to accomplish the organization's goals. Human skills allow a leader to assist group members in working cooperatively as a group to achieve common goals. Leaders with human skills create an atmosphere of trust. Being a leader with human skills means being sensitive to the needs and motivations of others and taking into account others' needs." The Behavioural Approach also emphasizes concern for people over results. Bob Chapman, CEO of Berry-Wehmiller suggests that one should treat employees as your family (Bob Chapman: Why You Should Treat Your Employees As Family, n.d.). Therefore, we can witness an evolution of human relationships in leadership theories surrounding family culture.

Earlier in chapter four, we have understood familyhood in detail. There we saw that we need to expand the territory of our sense of familyhood. Pramukh Swami Maharaj expanded his territory of familyhood that had no limits. After he renounced his family, he accepted the whole world as a family and every human being as his family members. On 17th August 1983, Swamiji was in Sarangpur, Gujarat, India. One night, he went for a walk, P. Santosh Bhagat asked him, "You are great, how are you so reachable to us?" Swamiji replied, "As a father talks to his son!" (Pramukh Charitam). People didn't know, but Swamiji's feelings were always like a father to his devotees. In 1990, youth from London said to Swamiji, "You are my good friend." Swamiji said, "Not only good friend, I am your good mentor and good father also." Once Swamiji told Brahmvihari Swami, "Mother's love is different, Father's love is different... but in Guru (Spiritual Leader/Mentor) it's all in one. A true leader can act upon every role – father, mother, brother, and friend" (Jeva Me Nirkhya Re - 7, 1995, p. 75).

The Merriam Webster dictionary defines family as, "A group of individuals living under one roof and usually under one head: household." Someone asked Swamiji, "What is your address?" Swamiji replied, "The whole world." Those who constrain themselves to few people as family, possess a small roof and have an address. But those who feel the whole world as their family, the limitless sky is their roof then there is no address. Once the sheikh of Bahrain inquired, "Where is your house?" Swamiji said, "I have no house. The whole world is my house." The sheikh delighted to hear that.

The second definition dictionary shows for the family is, "A group of persons of common ancestry." For Swamiji, we all belonged to the common ancestry – 'GOD.' That was the reason he understood the whole world as one family. On 16th April 2004, Swamiji was in New York. The state assemblyman of New York, David McDonnell expressed his feelings to Swamiji, "I highly appreciate and respect what you do in this world, especially for the poor. The way you have initiated the familyhood among people, I am deeply touched by it." Swamiji replied, "For GOD everyone is equal. None is rich or poor. All belongs to GOD – if we have this perspective, then we can act fair to all irrespective of differences. We all need to put effort into everyone's happiness" (Vicharan Report April 2004).

In London, there was a youth convention. Swamiji announced, "I love you all." When Prince Philip visited Akshardham, Gandhinagar, he asked volunteers, "Where is Pramukh Swami?" They answered, "Swamiji is in a small village near Surat to meet tribal families there." Prince Philip was amazed, "Oh! Swamiji built this marvelous palace and didn't stay here?" Pramukh Swamiji never stayed at palaces. He empathetically kept traveling to care and heal like a mother; support like a brother or friend; to take their responsibilities and counsel them like a father. He may become a Mother Teresa for the sick, Father of the nation Mahatma Gandhi to protect them & fight for their rights, their brother or a true friend to support them. It's a sense of familyhood for followers.

In this section, six characteristics of familyhood are explored: Personal care, Responsibility, Sacrifice, Emotional Support, Empathy, and Training. Many leadership styles weigh on human relationship, care for customers, care for employees, support to employees, applying emotional intelligence at workplace, training theories for subordinates and so on.

7th September 2007, Swamiji was in the US. After a Vedic Ritual, Swamiji addressed the assembly, "In Indian scriptures, it is said that the whole world is our family. We have learned it through the Vedas. If we believe it very firmly then we can seek inner peace. Everyone belong to our family, then for whom we can have envy or hatred? The familyhood leads us to no harm to anyone. It's a great idea" (Vicharan Report September 2007).

In the following chapters, we will see Swamiji had a greater picture of followers as a family, world as a family – therefore, he could act upon various roles. When it was required to care, he was a mother; to take responsibility, he was a father; to train others he was the best coach; to support he was an empathetic brother and everything we can think of! The following chapters in this section will strengthen our sense of familyhood and help us enlarge its periphery. One can get a lot of inspiration from a variety of incidences to change oneself. We learn by example, let's learn from Swamiji and cultivate a higher and broader sense of familyhood.

> "As with any journey, who you travel with can be more important than your destination."
>
> ~ iliketoquote.com ~

15. Personal Care

"Nobody cares how much you know, until they know how much you care."
~ Theodore Roosevelt

During the Vietnam War, a brother and sister of about 10 years of age were admitted to hospital. Their parents had been killed in an explosion, and the girl had been seriously injured. The doctors said that she needed blood. After blood tests, it was discovered that her brother had the same blood group. A nurse explained, "If you want your sister to live, you will have to give her your blood." The boy was willing. He was made to lie down on a bed, and a needle was inserted into his vein and blood was extracted. The boy could see the bottle next to his bed filling up with blood. The boy silently looked on. Then he called the nurse over and said, in a low voice, "Nurse, when do I die?" The boy didn't know that it wasn't necessary to die to give blood. But he was willing to die, to give up his own life for the sake of his sister. Yes, its familyhood that initiates us to care and sacrifice.

Mother Cares for Food

Devotees used to see Swamiji daily in the morning, afternoon and late evening. On October 2013, at 1.55 p.m., Swamiji returned to his room. His blood pressure was low, so he was given amla juice. Then Swamiji asked, "Has everyone had their meal?" An attendant sadhu replied, "Yes, everyone had lunch at noon." Swamiji asked, "Did we serve lunch to everyone?"

The attendant sadhus explained about the dining arrangements for the devotees, and that 3,000 devotees were served. Then Swamiji enquired about the dining arrangements of the sadhus. On hearing the details, Swamiji was satisfied.

Later, Swamiji asked the sadhus, "Have you all had lunch?" Everyone nodded saying, "We all had puranpoli, and Viveksagar Swami served us all today." Swamiji felt happy and praised, "The sadhus are all very good. They make proper arrangements and are meticulous in all seva" (Swaminarayan Bliss November, 2013).

Despite being 92 at the time, and with his health fluctuating, Swamiji's care for devotees and sadhus was unmatched. For many years Swamiji cooked food himself and served devotees earlier, so it was his daily quest whether everyone had their meal or not?

Mother Serves

Yogiji Maharaj was the spiritual leader of BAPS before Pramukh Swamiji. In 1970, Yogiji Maharaj was in London. By that time, a small follower's group had flourished. Everyone who came to meet him, Yogiji Maharaj denoted him 'President.'. Haka Khachar, an old devotee from India, was somewhat surprised. He asked, "How many presidents do you have in this small group?" Yogiji Maharaj replied, "Anyone who serves others is also a president" (Biography of Yogiji Maharaj).

In the past decade, the Service Principal has received a great deal of emphasis in leadership literature. It is evident in the writings of Block (1993), Covey (1990), De Pree (1989), Gilligan (1982), and Kouzes and Posner (1995), all of whom maintained that attending to others is the primary building block of moral leadership. Further emphasis on service can be observed in the work of Senge (1990) in his well-recognized writing on learning organizations. Senge contended that one of the essential tasks of leaders in learning organizations is to be the steward (servant) of the vision within the organization. Being a steward means clarifying and nurturing a vision that is greater than oneself. This means not being self-centered, but instead integrating one's self or vision with that of others in the organization. Effective leaders see their personal vision as an essential part of something larger than themselves—a part of the organization and the community at large. Bill George found that authentic leaders have a genuine desire to serve others (Northouse, Leadership: Theory and Practice, 2016, p. 197). Ethical leaders serve others by being altruistic, placing others' welfare ahead of their own in an effort to contribute to the common good (Northouse, Leadership: Theory and Practice, 2016, p. 359).

The idea of leaders serving others was more deeply explored by Robert Greenleaf (1970, 1977), who developed the servant leadership approach. Greenleaf said, "Servant leadership begins with the natural feeling that one wants to serve. Servant leaders make a conscious choice to serve first" (Northouse, Leadership: Theory and Practice, 2016, p. 253).

Mother to a child is the best servant leader. Servant leadership begins with the natural feeling that one wants to serve, to serve first. In Sarangpur during a quiz program, there was a question to Swamiji: "What do you want to become?" Swamiji's prompt answer was, 'Servant' (Kjdas, 1997).

In 1981, Swamiji was in Mount Abu. The driver of his car was cutting vegetables. Swamiji sat next to him and said, "Give me some partnership in this service." The driver said, "You are the leader. Stay sleeping partner with it." Swamiji replied, "Doing it on my own is a real partnership" (Divine Memories - 1, 1997).

Once in Calcutta, a devotee found that the tea he had been served was slightly bitter. When Swamiji came to know of this, he asked for some sugar. He personally placed it in the teacup and- with no spoon at hand - he dipped his finger in the tea and stirred it! On another occasion, to appease a crying baby, Swamiji placed his thumb in the baby's mouth! It did the trick. Yes, young or old, Swamiji understands (The Current Spiritual Guru Pramukh Swami Maharaj, n.d.).

It was 5th February 1965. There was a massive gathering from all around at Sarangpur. Swamiji retired managing things around 2 am to catch a couple of hours of sleep. The celebration of Shastirji Maharaj's birthday was on the next day. A few minutes later, a follower arrived from Nadiad. He was angry as there was no blanket or boarding facility for him. Devcharan Swami tried to calm him, but he was restless. Swamiji got up and patiently listened to him, and gave him his mattress, pillow, and blanket and said, "Here, take these and rest now" (Pramukh Swami Maharaj - Life & Work in Brief, 2013, p. 39).

Sadhu Narendraprasad Das recollects his fond memories with Swamiji while he served him during 1968-69. He was a student and staying in room no. 14 at Vidyanagar BAPS hostel. He recalls, "I was reading late one night when there was a knock at the door. It was open, so I didn't get up. Slowly the caller pushed it open, to my shock it was Pramukh Swamiji! They looked very tired from traveling. Swamiji saw the light from our room, and so, rather than wake others up he came to our room. My roommate and I jumped up and told, "We will just go and tell the hostel admin to make arrangements for you." Swamiji stopped us, "There's no need, let them sleep. We'll spend the night here in your room." So, we gave them bedding belonging to some students who had gone home. It was our regular time to prepare tea. Summoning up all my courage, I meekly asked Swamijshri, "We were going to make some hot milk, will you have some with us?" Swamiji replied, "Let me make it, let's see how it turns out." He went out onto our balcony and returned with cups in his hand. To our astonishment, he hadn't made hot milk. He had actually made tea for us! "It's tea!" exclaimed my roommate. "Swamiji how did you guess that we really wanted to drink tea?" I asked. "It's obvious isn't it," he answered softly. Then without taking anything else, he settled down on the bedding on the floor. "Swami, please. Sleep on the bed..." we begged. But he stayed on the floor, while we all slept in our beds — so much authority, and yet so unceremonious. Two years after that night, Swamiji said to me, "Until now you have been drinking tea, I think it's the time that you put an end to this habit too (Divine Memories - 2, 1997, p. 42).

Devcharan Swami, Swamiji's attendant reports, "There was a festival of "Jalzilani" in Sarangpur. That afternoon devotees finished lunch and left. When I get to Swamiji's bedroom, he was not there. I searched for him and found him cleaning the toilet blocks of devotees. Swamiji fetched water from the well, splash it across the floor and scrub it. I quickly ran to him and told, "Stop, don't do it, I will finish the rest." Swamiji enthusiastically said, "You fetch the water, and I'll scrub the floor. We two are better than one." So, Devcharan Swami fetched the water, and together they cleaned the entire area (Kpdas, Pramukhcharitramrut Sagar Part 2, 2009).

It was 5th May 1968. We were getting ready to leave Calcutta for Benares. As usual, I had to prepare a lunch pack for our travel. I started rolling the puris. The oil was sizzling, indicating it was ready for the puris to be fried. There was no one to help me fry them. Swamiji while passing by took a peek in. He understood the situation; I couldn't do both the jobs simultaneously. He was president of the organization. He could have sent for someone to help me. But he sought an empty kerosene can near the stove and sat down on it to start frying the puris. He was so relaxed about it: no fuss, no commotion (Divine Memories - 1, 1997, p. 86).

In Surat, a youngster Atul Mehta was sweeping the floor. Swamiji saw him doing it alone and said, "Atul, let me help you sweep. You are alone, but I am here with you" (Vicharan Report January 1985).

Swamiji was in Kantharia (A village near Limbadi) in 1967. His assistant Devcharan Swami was making 'Puri' for devotees, but there was no one to fry them. Pramukh Swamiji sat on a tin barrel and started frying the 'Puri.'

Mother Gives Priority to her Children

Greenleaf for a servant leader says, "Putting others first is the sine qua non of servant leadership—the defining characteristic. It means using actions and words that clearly demonstrate to followers that their concerns are a priority, including placing followers' interests and success ahead of those of the leader. It may mean a leader breaks from his or her tasks to assist followers with theirs.

The spiritual successor to Pramukh Swami Maharaj and current BAPS president Mahant Swami Maharaj often recalls an incidence with Pramukh Swamiji, "It was around 1950 when I was in Ahmedabad at Amlivali Pole. Babubhai Somnath had great attachment for the Sanstha. However, he seemed quite miserly. So much so that he provided essentials such as flour, ghee, and other cooking ingredients hesitatingly. But Swamiji, instead of becoming upset, was content with whatever Babubhai handed out. Swamiji would prepare our meals himself. Somehow, he had come to know that I have a preference for rotlis instead of rice. So, on a daily basis, he gave me his share of rotlis, even though we had to make do with a limited supply! He was content with other items such as dal and rice. In addition to all of this, he would spread all of the ghee on the rotlis so that I would find them more palatable, leaving none for him. He worked so subtly and silently that I never came to realize he was sacrificing so much for me. As I was young, I had a mighty appetite. Yet, my dilemma was that I felt a bit shy to ask for more; I felt very constrained. But Swamiji's love was such that it broke through all barriers. With constant affection, he would continue to serve me until I felt content. I didn't even have the common courtesy to inquire if there was anything left for Swamiji! Truly, even today, I relish the boundless and selfless love he showed. His has been a steady stream of love which continues to flow unceasingly to this day" (Kjdas, 1997).

Leaders place the good for followers over their own self-interests and emphasize follower development. Swamiji always sacrificed his comfort for the followers. Once a devotee Tulsibhai reported his problem to Swamiji, "I have just been operated for the cataract in my eyes. Right now, the spectacles I have are bulky; please send me lightweight spectacles." Swamiji instantly requested his attendant to give his own spectacles to Tulsibhai (Brahmopanishad, 1992, p. 60).

In 1965, there was a grand festival in Atladra. A devotee arrived 2 am. There were no more beddings left for him. Pramukh Swamiji noticed it and gave his own bedding to him (Pramukh Swami Maharaj - Life & Work in Brief, 2013, p. 39).

Sadhu Yagnavallabhdasji got emotional recalling an incidence, "After Swamiji's bypass surgery on 7th July 1998, we had an opportunity to meet Swamiji at the hospital on the 9th of July. Swamiji was sleeping, a vertical incision on his chest was stitched up with staples. There were electrodes and wires on his chest to monitor his heart function and medicines were being administered intravenously in his left hand. We got nervous about seeing Swamiji in such a condition. On seeing us, Dr. Kiranbhai Doshi from Mumbai, standing nearby, said to Swamiji, "Sadhus have come to see you."

Swamiji began to lovingly inquire about our health, looking at us as if we were very important. He looked at me and said, "Yagnavallabh has come." Then, on seeing Haridarshan Swami, he tried to lift his hand with intravenous tubes to bless him. On seeing Vivekmurti Swami, he said, "Bakul, you too have come?" Thus, Swamiji greeted us all, addressing us by our names.

Then he began to ask me, "Where have you come from?" I said, "Bapa! From New York mandir."

Bapa said, "Are all the devotees well and happy."

"Yes, Bapa," I said.

It was only the second day after the bypass surgery. A patient's lungs become weak due to bypass surgery, and he can barely speak. Yet, Swamiji was speaking. So, we said, "Bapa! Now, don't speak. Take rest." Then we came out and went to Thakorji's room. Some sadhus had tears in their eyes. All the sadhus became emotional. Any patient in this condition would feel drowsy because of the medicine. He would not think of anything except his pain, while we found that Swamiji had transcended bodily pain and discomfort. Not only that, he was lovingly inquiring about the health of his sadhus and devotees" (Swaminarayan Bliss, Nov-Dec , 2012).

Swamiji was so attached to his devotees; he even forgot his illness. Once Dr. Dixit was to take his teeth X-ray. He was adjusting his X-ray machine. Swamiji was busy reading letters. When called, he reached the X-ray machine reading letter in his hands. After the X-ray, he instantly continued with it (Brahmopanishad, 1992, p. 184). He always thought of what can I do for others? What is the maximum that I can give out of myself? Once he said to some sadhus, "All of you have renounced home & family to please Yogiji Maharaj. I have a constant feeling what can I do for you? Let this body perish in service to all of you. Whenever you need me, don't hesitate. I am available even at midnight. You can wake me up for any of your needs or problems"

(Pramukh Charitam).

When there is an event of honor for a person, he forgets everything but himself. For Swamiji the reverse was right, he forgot himself concerning others. In Limbadi there was an event to honor Swamiji. While everyone was praising him, he was busy writing answers to devotees. The moment the mayor came to garland and present the memento he stopped for a while, received the memento and the very next second continued with letters — no quest for photographs, acclamation or selfie (Brahmopanishad, 1992, p. 184).

Sincere Servant

Swamiji was so honest and sincere with his services that a Muslim, Madam Mohammed wrote a letter to Swamiji in 1992 when he heard Swamiji was ill. That was around the time of Yogiji Maharaj's centenary festival. With a remark 'Pending' Swamiji's letter writing assistant stored it aside. After 18 years a sadhu found it unattended and gave it to Swamiji. Swamiji insisted on calling Madam Mohammed. Volunteers inquired about the address but learned that he had moved. Swamiji emphasized that the search must continue and after two days, Madam Mohammed arrived to meet him. The man was brought to tears to think that Swamiji had not forgotten him and sought him 18 years later (Vicharan Report February 2010, p. 25)! Despite Swamiji receiving 1500-2000 letters a month, he was very loyal and faithful to attend and answer every single letter to the best of his ability. For him, the letter writing was not a job but devotion and love for people.

Once a devotee Reshma Pargi from a tribal village 'Poshina' wrote a letter. The public handpump at his village stopped working. The letter reached Swamiji in the US. The handwriting was so bad, Swamiji spent ten minutes but could not interpret it. Reading the postage mark, he gathered that the letter had come from Himmatnagar, India. Swamiji contacted Srirang Swamiji there to inquire who wrote this letter and the meaning of it? After running a series of inquiries as to who sent the letter, the message was deciphered as coming from a tribal man called Reshma. He had written a letter that the handpump in his village was out of order. To repair the handpump, was the government's job, but Swamiji made the necessary arrangements to solve the issue. Swamiji could easily have spent time on organizational growth instead of listening and solving insignificant problems. But for him, people were a top priority. He never compromised people's need over his personal interests. In fact, he never had any personal interests; people were his interest and focus. He lived every moment of his life for people having no holidays or Sundays for his entire life.

Care is not only the way a mother holds her baby, while singing a lullaby to him and putting him to sleep, but it's also about the sacrifices the mother will make throughout her life to ensure that her child has everything that they truly need – timely and wholesome meals, an organized and clean room, words of support and motivation. Care is about how the mother always keeps an open ear for her child – ready to hear their sorrows and wipe their tears.

A Great Listener

Greenleaf pointed out listening as a characteristic of a servant leader. He said that a servant leader being receptive to what others have to say communicate by listening first, it's an interactive process of sending and receiving messages. Through listening, servant leaders acknowledge the viewpoint of followers and validate these perspectives (Northouse, Leadership: Theory and Practice, 2016).

Pramukh Swami Maharaj used to speak less and listen more. On an average, he used to meet 100 to 500 people daily, sometimes more than 1000 in a day. On 1st Feb 2005, he met 2025 people face to face and attended to each one for their problems. On 26th July 2004, he continuously sat from 4.30 to 8.30pm to meet people. He met people face to face, listened to their personal, family, financial, social, moral and spiritual problems and counseled them.

Swamiji treated every individual for their intrinsic value. He met and served everyone. Regardless of the person being a Prime minister or someone from a lower socio-economic background, regardless of how much someone contributed to BAPS, it was all irrelevant. He served one and all the same.

On 29th November 2005 in Jaipur, a man was waiting in the queue to meet Swamiji. Though Swamiji didn't understand English, this man started a long talk. After a few minutes, Swamiji requested him to speak in Hindi. Despite knowing Hindi, he continued in English. There was nothing significant or relevant in his talk. People were getting irritated and tried to stop him wasting Swamiji's time. Swamiji continued to listen to him till the end with patience just as he would be if he were listening to a dignitary giving a speech (Vicharan Report November 2005). For Swamiji, every human being was unique and respectful. He saw everyone as divine irrespective of their outer perception, post, education, wealth, behavior or contribution to the BAPS organization.

Another way he listened to people was through letters. His followers wrote more than 5.5 lac (550,000+) letters to him. He responded to each one of them. There was an average of 50 letters per day he read and answered. The phone counseling was too many to count. He listened to and counseled more than 800,000 people after he became a spiritual successor (Socio Spiritual Works, n.d.).

On 8th August 2004, Swamiji was in Chicago. It was time to rest, so his attendant requested him to quit reading letters. Swamiji nodded because it was a 15-page A4 size letter. He read every page and answered it (Vicharan Report August 2004).

On 4th June 2010, a teenager wrote a 39-page letter to him. After reading the letter with patience, Swamiji called him. The teenager was very surprised, and he asked, "You read the entire letter, really?" Swamiji replied, "If I did not, how will I offer you a solution" (Vicharan Report June 2010)? Reading the problems of others, every single day for some many years for no material gain shows Swamiji's love and empathy for people.

On 3rd September 2011, Swamiji was in Mumbai and suffered severe pain due to blood clots in his eyes. He was unable to open his eyes, and therefore, it was impossible to read the letters that day. Dharmcharan Swamiji was called upon by Swamiji, and he was asked to read the letters out loud. Swamiji replied to those letters verbally (Vicharan Report September 2011).

On 18th July 2012 while he was answering letters, all of a sudden there was a blood flow from his nose. After Yogicharan Swami treated him, he continued as if nothing had happened (Vicharan Report July, 2012).

In July 2011 in Bharuch, Swamiji suffered a severe heart attack. Numerous medical apparatuses were continuously monitoring his heart. In those crucial moments, he worried for people and pleaded to the doctors, "Let Dharmcharan Swamiji read aloud the letters and let me answer those." The doctors were stunned at his plea and had to deny his request as his health and recovery were the top priority for them (Vicharan Report July, 2011).

Mother Never Tires

For a mother, there is no holiday or vacation when it comes to serving or caring for her children. She enjoys doing it for her child. Even if she falls sick, she always thinks of her child. She never gets tired of it or feels bored. Her care for her child is selfless.

In Mombasa, on 29th May 2007, Kiranbhai Patel said, "Swamiji, look the ocean is there, cool air is flowing. Yagnesh has built a beach house here. You may rest here. Treat it as a vacation. You may relax here for some days. Swamiji didn't like it and said, "I am always relaxed. Meeting people, listening to their problems, engaging myself in uplifting others, rests me. I never need a vacation. Every day is a holiday I enjoy" (Vicharan Report May 2007).

On 10th July 2005 in Mumbai, a child presented a rosary to Swamiji and demanded that he complete one round of the rosary. Despite a long queue behind, Swamiji fulfilled his wish and garlanded it to his neck (Vicharan Report July 2005).

He didn't deny visitors even after he was advised to rest after a heart attack at AIMS, Baroda. Once in Ahmedabad Swamiji said, "I am ready to listen to any sort of problems even at midnight. I never get tired of it. I know people feel comfortable explaining their problems to me" (Pramukh Charitam, 1990).

We can only imagine what people sought from him from the letter they wrote, their visits, and the phone calls. People trusted Swamiji that he could provide solutions and prayers for their problems or concerns.

In 1981, Swamiji was in Boston, USA. "Yesterday it was 2.30 am when Swamiji returned. So, it was time for him to rest. But he wrote letters for 2 hours because someone was going to India. Swamiji was to hand him over the letters to save the postage charges and delay (Pramukh Charitam, 1990).

On 26th March 2001, Anandjivan Swamiji asked, "Don't you get tired of letters?" Swamiji replied, "I am fortunate to serve people through this." It shows the glory he felt serving people (Vicharan Report March 2001).

Overlooking his pain and health, he often continued his routine letter reading and writing job. He strictly followed the principle of completing daily jobs the same day. He was so sympathetic to people; he felt the pain of others as his own. He worried more for people than himself. Someone asked Swamiji, 'Why do you keep answering the letters till midnight?' Swamiji replied, "People write their problems and await the response. It's my duty to send the reply as soon as possible."

On 7th April 2004, while Swamiji was on the way from the airport traveling in a car to his destination, Bandish Ajmera commented, "For the last hour you are reading a book-sized letter. Don't you feel exasperated? How do you not get energy and have the patience for it?" Swamiji replied, "I am never annoyed. I keep reading in a car, train, and airplane." It was astonishing that whenever he had time, he used to start reading letters. We could find him reading letters early in the morning or up late at night, and even during assemblies (Vicharan Report April 2004).

Once Sarvamangal Swami asked him in Sarangpur, "Don't you feel boredom reading tens of miserable letters every day?" Swamiji replied, "Never. I enjoy attending and serving people. It's my service to them" (Brahmopanishad, 1992, p. 207).

On 6th May 1984, he read letters continuously for 5 hours during his flight from the US to London (Pramukh Charitam). Years later, and his habit had not changed. On 5th April 2001, during his travel from Mumbai to Dubai, he read letters for two and a half hours non-stop with the same concentration and enthusiasm since he started writing the letters (Vicharan Report April 2001).

People who work for material gain don't enjoy their deeds. They get irritated of it. One who knows the value of selfless service enjoys its fruits from within. The external world can't enjoy them. They rest on the pious beach of selfless services. One who is ego-free and serves others just to serve, no desire for fame or anything else never get tired of their working hours, needs no vacation or relaxing activities. GOD gifts them everlasting inner joy, where they enjoy endlessly.

Open-Hearted, No Discrimination

Swamiji was above discrimination of caste, religion or country. He could help, serve and care for anyone he met.

In 2006 there was a flood in Surat (a city in Gujarat, India). Water rolled over and smashed the city. BAPS volunteers were in action and serving food packets and relief kits. Over the phone, Swamiji insisted to the volunteers, "Take care for all equally. Don't discriminate among our followers and non-followers."

In 1974, Welwyn Garden City, Hertfordshire, England. Swamiji went for lunch at Chandubhai's house. Chandubhai's old neighbor Mr. Stringer was a widower, and his sons had left him alone to live in miserable conditions. Swamiji asserted Chandubhai to take care of him. Mr. Stringer was touched that an unacquainted Hindu leader was taking up the duty of his sons! After 10 years, in 1984 when Swamiji once again visited London, Mr. Stringer met Swamiji and said, "Since that day, Chandubhai is taking care of me" (Anandswaroopdas, 1998).

There is often a question which arises. What is it about Swamiji that young children are drawn to him like metal to a magnet? On seeing Swamiji, the children erupt with joy.

Thousands of children of the BAPS Children's Wing worldwide have experienced Swamiji's, selfless love. Swamiji's heart is forever open to them all. For decades, Swamiji's routine was such that during his meals, he would sometimes engage in discussions with children and youths. They would receive inspiration and guidance. Seeing the freestyle interaction between Swamiji and the children convinces one that he holds no barriers or distinctions. There is no generation gap, for they all experience his genuine, selfless motherly love (Swaminarayan Bliss Nov-Dec, 2015).

Care is not only about the birthday gifts (which we like so much) and family portraits (where everyone is wearing their best clothes and showing a lot of teeth). It doesn't matter whether you're talking about a relationship between a father and son, two brothers, a husband and wife, and so on. Care is not just about the outside things, but it's something more profound. It's about the things you get as the result of the relationship, but it's about the care and the sacrifice that an individual makes for another.

> "The leaders who get most out of their people are the leaders who care most about their people."
>
> ~ Simon Sinek ~

16. Responsibility

"Action springs not from thought, but from a readiness for responsibility."
~ Dietrich Bonhoeffer ~

A father returned home only to get busy with work. He had brought some work files home. His son walked into the study and was distracting the father. The father played a trick to occupy his son so that he would not disturb him. There was a large world map hanging on the wall. He pulled it down from the wall. The father tore the map into many pieces. He asked his son to join the pieces together. The father assumed the son would take hours to fix it while he could work peacefully. In fact, within a few minutes, the map was joined up again. His father was stunned to see it and asked, "How could you do it so fast?" The boy turned the map around. At the back of the map was an image of a man. The boy said, when you were tearing the map, I noticed the image of the man. All I did was join the man back together.

Hitler caused a great catastrophe in the world. A single terrorist can disturb the entire nation & the world. Pramukh Swami Maharaj's philosophy was straightforward – instead of focusing more on a problem, focus more on the person. A person is the most basic unit of society, a group of several persons is called a family, bigger than this is a community, larger still is a nation, and at last, the world. If the smallest unit is perfect, then the family-community-nation and the world eventually become perfect.

Stogdill's second survey based on situational leadership points to 10 leadership characteristics. Topmost is the drive for responsibility and task completion. Responsibility to a leader doesn't allow any excuse; they need to manage it irrespective of circumstances and resources (Virkus, 2009).

Pramukh Swamiji had the drive for responsibility. He took the responsibility of carving human beings up to perfection. Parents take on a huge responsibility to nurture their child, feeding them, and providing necessities of life. The government takes on the responsibility to provide infrastructure, education, social security, food, etc. But there may be very few taking responsibilities to develop their people in all aspects of life. Swamiji took on the responsibility of his followers to develop all aspects of their life and built an infrastructure for this. He set an example for the rest of the world to follow. He did it very successfully. How he did and what was involved will be explored in the 'Development of People' section.

"We never fail when we try to do our duty, we always fail when we neglect to do it."

~ Robert Baden-Powell ~

17. Sacrifice

"She taught me all about real sacrifice. That it should be done from love... That it should be done from necessity, not without exhausting all other options.... who need your strength because they don't have enough of their own"
~ Veronica Roth, Allegiant ~

The leader is one who steps ahead to sacrifice himself/herself. This is one of the most fundamental differences in leaders and non-leaders. The leaders sacrifice their comforts, career, family life, higher positions, handsome earnings for the common good of the community. Non-leaders find it hard to sacrifice, but leaders come forward and contribute themselves adequately for the mission. They donate themselves for a noble cause.

Donated Himself

Swamiji often said, "I have donated myself to all of you as we don't wish the donated thing back and don't bother how others use it. I don't care for this body. It's for others now." This is how he lived his entire life. He gave himself to others, never expecting anything in return.

Bryant McGill in 'Voice of Reason' says, *"Giving yourself is the ultimate revolution."* Many devotees have witnessed it personally. In 2011, an ant was climbing up Swamiji's arm. Narayancharandas Swami saw the ant and came forward to remove it. Swamiji stopped him and said, "Don't remove, it has rights over me" (Narayancharandas, Brahmsannidhi, 2011). Thus, Swamiji always thought himself the property of every living creature. That was the reason anyone could see him without any prior appointment with no constraints of any protocol. It was astonishing that people compromised Swamiji's rest time, even when he had returned from long journeys. Still, he was there for them.

In 1991 Swamiji was in Mehsana. He had sat down for lunch. Food had been served in his wooden bowl, and there was a long-distance call for him. The conversation dragged on for many minutes. By the time it ended the chapatti had turned dry. Swamiji took a piece, but Krishnavallabh Swami told him to leave it since a fresh, hot one was being made. Swamiji replied that the one in his bowl would do. "One should learn to make do with whatever one gets," he added (Viveksagardas, 1997).

A group of devotees from Nani Vavdi were on a pilgrimage. They met Swamiji on the occasion of a vast assembly arranged by Pujya Pandurang Athvale in Allahabad. The organizer of their package tour had promised food, but he had changed his mind. In Allahabad, the devotees ran out of whatever stock they had brought with them. Since they did not eat hotel food, they were worried as to how they would manage for the rest of the pilgrimage. When Swamiji came to know of this, he knew that they had stock for five days. So, he called the attendant sadhus and told them, "Set aside enough food for Thakorji and give the rest to the devotees!" Without even harboring a thought of how he and the sadhus would fare, Swamiji allayed the fears of the devotees (Viveksagardas, 1997).

In Illness

Peter S. Beagle in his book 'The Last Unicorn' highlights, *"Real magic can never be made by offering someone else's liver. You must tear out your own, and not expect to get it back."* Pramukh Swamiji tore out himself for others.

Here are some incidences from the book 'Immortal River' by Viveksagar Swamiji:

Swamiji was in a village in Vasad, Gujarat, India. That day he had a high temperature of 102 degrees. He still visited 110 homes. And when Swami was in New York, a youth asked Swami to put on his slippers. He put them on the wrong way around. He told Atmaswarup Swami he couldn't see the slippers, never mind the slippers; later Swamiji told the sadhus that he couldn't recognize which sadhu it was - he only recognized them by their voice. Viveksagar Swami asked Swamiji, "Why didn't you inform us." Swamiji replied, "If I did, then we would have had to cancel meeting the devotees of America." He was prepared to lose his sight for his devotees.

On 13th January 1986, Swamiji was in Bhadra. He had a tumor, and it would need to be operated, but before the operation, he went to Gondal, Rajkot, and Sarangpur. He traveled to the villages of Kutch and then went to Mumbai. From Mumbai, he went to Delhi. There, he met President Dr. Zail Singh and then to a function held by Pandurang Aathavaleji in Allahabad. The journey continued to Calcutta where he met a few of his devotees before coming back to Bombay – where he had his operation on 11th April 1886. He had continued traveling for 4 months before being operated on.

Once Dr. Madhubhai Patel of Ahmedabad was taking a cardiogram of Swamiji. On reading the result, he cautioned, "Swamiji, don't exert yourself. This time the cardiogram is showing a slightly abnormal result. It seems you have strained quite a bit during your winter travels." Swamiji simply smiled. Once, Dr. Bhuva arrived from Bhavnagar to Sarangpur to report on Swamiji's health. He spoke solemnly to Swamiji, "The report shows lateral extension, meaning that the circulation in your heart has decreased a little. If this damage continues then your heart's function will decrease. You are going through a sensitive period; you must alter your routine." Swamiji simply smiled in return and kept his travel schedules intact.

As a consequence, on 5th February 1983, in Sundelpura, Swamiji suddenly felt an intolerable pain in his chest. It was a severe heart attack. After prompt medication, it was decided to take him to Vadodara by road. On the way, his car stopped at a crossroad. Those following Swamiji's car were anxious as to why the car had stopped. Everyone rushed to Swamiji's car. Swamiji called Acharya Swami and said to him, "I have stopped the car to tell you that today we were scheduled to give a discourse on the Shikshapatri at Dayabhai Gajjar's home in Anand. But now that I'm sick, I'll not be able to go. He must have made all the arrangements and invited his friends and relatives. Go directly to Anand with a couple of sadhus and deliver the discourse." It's incredible that in spite of his critical health, Swamiji was thinking about his schedule at a devotee's home. To avoid any disturbance in plans and disappointment on the part of the devotee he made the arrangements. It's impossible to think of someone else when one is in such a critical situation

Swamiji was at Himatnagar in 1989. A sudden bout of fever, diarrhea, and vomiting left him weak. At 1.30 p.m. a discussion followed with regards to canceling all his programmes and returning to Ahmedabad for rest and treatment. To this Swamiji asserted, "If you want me to rest then we can go ahead to Khedbrahma and rest there. What is wrong with that? So many devotees are waiting for us..." Eventually, on the doctor's advice, Swamiji returned to Ahmedabad. Swamiji's insistence on pleasing the devotees in spite of his fever and poor health reveals his spirit of tolerance and compassion (Viveksagardas, 1997).

Swamiji's constant travels and his will to bear all hardships have always been a cause of worry and concern for his doctors. Once, when Swamiji was in Sarangpur, several doctors, namely, Dr. Samani, Dr. Kiran Doshi, Dr. Panchal, and Dr. Bhagubhai Patel, came from Mumbai to check on his health. Regarding the lateral extension, Dr. Samani advised, "Swami! The heart is a muscle. It requires a large amount of blood, and therefore God has equipped it with more than one artery. But if one of them becomes blocked, then it will receive less blood. And so, the chances of damage to the heart increases. So, you should keep your health in mind while serving the Sanstha." To this Swamiji replied with silence and a smile.

After a diagnosis like this, anyone else would have thought twice about climbing or getting down even two steps. But Swamiji took the warning lightly and blessed the doctor. For the sake of pleasing the devotees and fulfilling their wishes, Swamiji has always been indifferent to his health.

Once, Swamiji completed the home visits in Piplag and arrived in Dabhan. A short while later devotees from Piplag came to Swamiji and said a few homes had been left out. Swami went back to Piplag, visited the devotees' homes and returned to Dabhan around midnight. On another occasion Swamiji left Badalpur, covering thirteen villages and visiting 50 homes before reaching Anand at midnight. In the hilly, undulating land of Badalpur Swamiji visited the homes of devotees by walking distances of up to two kilometers from morning till evening. The hollows and hills in Bamangam village would tire and exhaust even a sturdy youth. Swamiji, without a whisper of complaint, sanctified fifty homes (Viveksagardas, 1997)!

Compromising Schedules

Swamiji's vicharan schedule had been usually preplanned for two to three months. But many times, his devotees demanded his time and visits, and they would disturb his pre-planning. Once a little boy urged Swamiji to visit his village. It could cause a significant disturbance to Swamiji' schedule, but Swamiji agreed.

On 1st May 1977, Swamiji arrived at Ganesh's village Kankaravadi. He was to reside at Nanjibhai's simple house. The house did not have electricity, a toilet or bathroom. The evening assembly was under the light of a paraffin lamp. As even basic facilities were not available, Swamiji stayed there so delighted as if he had come to attend a festival (Swaminarayan Bliss, Nov-Dec, 2012).

In 1989, Swamiji left by road from Sankari to Bhaatiyar. The road was rough and rugged. Ghelakaka, a devotee, was on his deathbed. It was his dying wish that Swamiji should perform his last rites. The village, for this reason, was going to see Swamiji for the first time. But before Swamiji arrived heavy rains had flooded the main lanes and courtyards of the village. He reached the house of Ghelakaka with some difficulty. The blind old man was seated by the entrance door, waiting for Swamiji. Swamiji called out and said, "Jai Swaminarayan." The old man was overwhelmed.

Sacrificed Comforts

Even though we have many beautiful mandirs, Swamiji is always on the move. He never stays in any one of the mandirs for long. Each day there's a new village to visit. The drinking water changes, people are different, and the conditions vary too. Yet, he moves with joy; unruffled by the changing environments and situations. Once in Naika, Brahmavihari Swami asked him, "Are you comfortable in this small congested room?" "I am comfortable everywhere. I do not come from a royal family," and then Swamiji added, "I come from a farmer's background. Before I became a sadhu, I used to tend to cows" (Viveksagardas, 1997).

Whenever Swamiji traveled by train at night, the devotees unfailingly greeted him at each station. He never got fed up of standing by the compartment door or, if there was time, in addressing the devotees on the platform. All this he did at the cost of his rest hours. And so, in spite of getting little sleep or rest, Swamiji was happy. Swamiji had traveled happily and with ease in a bullock cart, camel cart, horse-drawn buggy, rickshaw, tractor, truck, railway maintenance car, 3rd class train compartment, car, helicopter, and plane. His joy remained undiminished, regardless of the vehicle he traveled in. A devotee in Bhadra inquired, "Why didn't you use a helicopter? We can arrange it for you." "A Maruti car or a helicopter– both are equal in our eyes. The same applies to a hut or a palace." Swamiji's reply was spontaneous. At another time, Swamiji said, "If I just fly in helicopters then small villages will be left, and only cities will be covered" (Viveksagardas, 1997).

Swamiji was in the city of Selvas, Gujarat, in 1973. He was at the home of a devotee, Ranjitsinh Chauhan. A poor tribal boy, Rambhai Makanji Patel, studying in Grade 9 came for his darshan. He asked, "Will you come to my house?" The devotees explained that the boy's village, Moti Tambadi, was inaccessible by car. Swamiji was touched by the boy's love and feelings and said, "Our car will go. We will come!" The boy felt very happy. The rough road made the ride bumpy and uncomfortable. And he completed the final leg of his journey by bullock cart to fulfill the wish of the poor boy.

Once, some sadhus were casually talking with Swamiji in Bhadra. Someone said, "There are no bathrooms or toilets in Dangra. One has to go in the open." Swamiji replied, "In Atladra we had to walk a good distance to the outskirts of the village! Once I had a bout of diarrhea, and I had to stay there for half an hour. In those days there were no toilet facilities." Recalling his days in Sarangpur, he once said, "In the days when I was the Kothari of Sarangpur, we all used to go to bathe by the riverbank. Many years later, when I was no longer the Kothari, makeshift toilets of jute cloth with no roof on top were made" (Viveksagardas, 1997). Such were the conditions for even the President of a worldwide organization.

In Gajera, Swamiji's residence and the venue for the daily discourses were adjacent to each other. Each day, the devotees attending the discourses had to catch the 5.45 p.m. bus to return to their neighboring villages. Keeping this in mind, the afternoon discourse was scheduled to start at 3.30 p.m. Someone suggested that the time be changed to a later hour to avoid disturbing Swamiji's afternoon sleep. To this Swamiji replied, "There is no need for that because the devotees will not get another bus to get home." Swamiji has always changed his schedules or put up with disturbances to suit the convenience of the devotees (Viveksagardas, 1997).

In many villages, despite the lack of essential amenities and other issues, Swamiji had remained undeterred and unflappable in his vicharan[3]. When he traveled in the Bhal region, he remained calm and happy, but those accompanying him became frustrated and irritated. The reason being that the region challenged them like no other place: they had to put up with drinking the murky and salty waters of the village pond, the scorching sun, absence of electric lights and fans and the assault of dust particles saturating the air! To add to these difficulties, every village carried out a procession to honor Swamiji. This further created clouds of dust. Then, invariably, a Satsang assembly followed by visits to follower's houses. But Swamiji never complained or became agitated. The stories of Swamiji's arduous and historical vicharan in thousands of villages and towns will forever remain etched in the annals of history. However, the notable fact of it all is that Swamiji had never mentioned or complained about his hardships (Swaminarayan Bliss Nov-Dec, 2015)!

He traveled to villages and cities, farms and fields, homes and huts; sanctifying and blessing ceaselessly. He had reached out to countless people to dissolve their pains and celebrate their joys. He sacrificed himself in the midst of society to resolve its sufferings and calamities. His attitude of making do with whatever accommodation and food he gets are similarly reflected in his travels. When traveling by train, he always preferred to travel by third class. He has used bullock carts while going from one village to another. In cities, he has often traveled to devotees' homes in horse-drawn buggies and rickshaws. In all the modes of travel and situations, his spiritual happiness has always remained undisturbed.

His unique character as a spiritual traveler was striving his utmost to uplift all. A candle sacrifices it giving light to others; a rose turn to dust to please others with its fragrance, the leaders also enlighten and blossom others sacrificing themselves.

---

[3] Vicharan is spiritual travel for the purpose of transmitting moral and spiritual inspiration. It is the tradition of personally visiting devotees in their villages, towns and cities.

Complete Leadership

"Real leaders are not blinded by the trappings of power but recognize their role as servant."
~ Archbishop Desmond Tutu ~

18. Emotional Support

"You can't move up in the staircase of leadership unless you are emotionally intelligent."
~ Amit Ray ~

Human beings are not machines. The emotions drive their mood, activities, decisions, and performance. Therefore, a leader should provide emotional support to their followers. A leader needs to keep the team members motivated, energetic, and working up to their full potential. Greenleaf in Servant Leadership had highlighted 'Emotional Healing.' He said, "Emotional Healing is sensitive to the personal concerns and well-being of others. It includes recognizing others' problems and being willing to take the time to address them. A servant leader is available to others, stand by them and provide them with support." (Northouse, Leadership: Theory and Practice, 2016, p. 234). Pramukh Swami Maharaj on an average spent an hour daily for his followers to provide them with emotional support.

Sometimes people who possess intellect brilliance with vast experience and education lead to emotional disasters among their followers to a work culture with low creativity, lack of enthusiasm, lower productivity, and fear (Lynn, 2000). A discouraging factor against performance is depression.

People with depression usually have several of the following: a loss of energy; a change in appetite; sleeping more or less; anxiety; reduced concentration; indecisiveness; restlessness; feelings of worthlessness, guilt, or hopelessness; and thoughts of self-harm or suicide. Low levels of recognition and access to care for depression and another common mental disorder, anxiety, result in a global economic loss of a trillion US dollars every year. The losses are incurred by households, employers, and governments. Households lose out financially when people cannot work. Employers suffer when employees become less productive and are unable to work. Governments have to pay higher health and welfare expenditures ("Depression: let's talk says WHO, as depression tops list of causes of ill health, n.d.).

W.H.O. has announced depression a most considerable factor to affect performance. The WHO Director-General, Dr. Margaret Chan said, "These new figures are a wake-up call for all countries to re-think their approaches to mental health and to treat it with the urgency that it deserves" (Depression, n.d.).

In many countries, there is no, or very little, support available for people with mental health disorders. Even in high-income countries, nearly 50% of people with depression do not get treatment. On average, just 3% of government health budgets is invested in mental health, varying from less than 1% in low-income countries to 5% in high-income countries ("Depression: let's talk says WHO, as depression tops list of causes of ill health, n.d.).

In 2017 WHO lead a global campaign 'Depression' for a year. Dr. Shekhar Saxena, Director of the Department of Mental Health and Substance Abuse at WHO said, "One of the first steps is to address issues around prejudice and discrimination. The continuing stigma associated with mental illness was the reason why we decided to name our campaign Depression. For someone living with depression, talking to a person they trust is often the first step towards treatment and recovery" ("Depression: let's talk says WHO, as depression tops list of causes of ill health, n.d.).

A great advantage with Pramukh Swami Maharaj was his availability for such issues. People trusted him sharing their personal problems related to depression or suicide. Swamiji could pacify thousands of people through his kind and encouraging guidance.

Here are some examples of his grace in handling such personal problems:

A depressed youth came to Swamiji, "I have no work. I am not worthy of living in the world ...." His thoughts led him to think everyone was selfish and worthless. He lost interest in life. Swamiji encouraged him, "The mercy of God and Saint is up to you. So, you have to move forward. Kick off the negative beliefs and think positive. No one is useless in this world. Other people can perform why can't you? You are as equal as others. You don't know the power and force in yourself. It takes time, but efforts always payback. If someone falls, he gets up and starts again. You need to stand up and start moving ahead. If there is an error, one should correct it. Now, forget everything and plan for future (Yauvan na Suhrad, p. 89). Swamiji enlightened a diminishing lamp and recharged the youth with hope and energy during a short conversation.

Especially when long-lasting and with moderate or severe intensity, depression may become a serious health condition. It can cause the affected person to suffer greatly and function poorly at work, at school, and in the family. At its worst, depression can lead to suicide. Close to 800,000 people die due to suicide every year. Suicide is the second leading cause of death in 15-29-year-olds (Depression, n.d.).

A youth trapped in an awkward situation met Swamiji in Atladra. His business partner cheated him. As a consequence, he started drinking alcohol and tried to kill his partner. When his father brought him to Swamiji, he was restless and, ignoring his father when his father tried to speak to him.

Swamiji said, "The business will settle down again. We will pray on your behalf. Be stable, do not panic or do any harm to anyone. Drinking alcohol all day is not going to solve the problem. It only leads rise to family conflicts and causes harm to your body. If you work hard, then things will settle. Decide first what you want to do, then you won't find time to think the past incidences, and thus the tension will go away" (Yauvan na Suhrad, p. 48) Swamiji's advice worked and within few days the youth was back on track.

Depression may lead to drug addiction. According to the National Survey on Drug Use and Health (NSDUH), 21.5 million American adults (aged 12 and older) battled a substance use disorder in 2014. The Substance Abuse and Mental Health Services Administration (SAMHSA) shows that in 2014, almost 8 million American adults battled both a mental health disorder and a substance use disorder, or co-occurring disorders. Drug abuse and addiction cost American society close to $200 billion in healthcare, criminal justice, legal, and lost workplace production/participation costs in 2007, the Office of National Drug Control Policy (ONDCP) reports. The World Health Organization (WHO) estimates the global burden of disease related to drug and alcohol issues to be 5.4 percent worldwide (Thomas, n.d.).

During Swamiji's stay at New York, a drug addict met Swamiji. He was distressed and felt lonely. He said, "I am going through a difficult time." Swamiji lovingly told him, "Why did you start drugs? People have misguided you, at such a young age how can there be difficulties?"

With a heavy tone, the addict replied, "Swamiji, I am getting bored." Swamiji exclaimed, "Bored! Bored of what? You have a healthy body, working hands, legs, quite young. Why distress? Why can't you control it? Believe in God and praise him, you will definitely overcome it."

As Swamiji was said this, new energy started flowing in his eyes. He said, "Swamiji, I sought wisdom here. So far, no one has been able to understand me. They talked about their selfish intentions. Only you have explained to me about God and solutions." He was happy as Swamiji diagnosed him accurately and cured him accordingly.

An elderly man came to Swamiji on 10th September 2008. He was mentally disturbed and unfortunate. Due to depression, he jumped from the ninth floor to commit suicide but survived, with some minor injuries. He was also suffering from urinal inflammation. He complained, "This is the reason I wanted to die." Swamiji counseled, "Will it solve the problem? Pray to GOD. He will help you come out of it" (Vicharan Report September 2008).

On 22nd September 2003 Sarangpur in Sarangpur, a devotee brought his son to meet Swamiji. He won a gold medal in M.Sc. He wanted to do a Ph.D. but was stuck due to depression. Swamiji asked, "What's the reason behind it?" He said, "I want to become the richest man like Dhirubhai Ambani." Swamiji understood that the youth was trying to reach out to achieve something but did not have the burning desire within. Swamiji said, "It's not a one day job. You can excel gradually. Right now, start your studies. Work hard. Growth is a step by step progress" (Vicharan Report September 2003).

On 25th of January 2005 in Surat, a youngster came to Swamiji. One of his family members had criticized him, and he had swallowed poison pills. He survived. Swamiji said, "Never repeat it again. Your family members criticized you so that you could improve and become a better person. Why do you get so tense? Those who criticize, you should think good for them. Pray before God to help you and bless you with strength" (Vicharan Report January 2005).

Thoughts of wisdom can fade out depressive thoughts. Swamiji, a man of wisdom, could easily kick sadness, depression and negative thoughts.

> "Courage is what it takes to stand up and speak; courage is also what it takes down to listen."
>
> ~ Winston Churchill ~

19. Empathy

"If you can't have empathy and have effective relationships, then no matter how smart you are, you are not going to get very far."
~ Daniel Goleman ~

Standing in Others' Shoes

Empathy is "standing in the shoes" of another person and attempting to see the world from that person's point of view. Empathetic servant leaders demonstrate that they genuinely understand what followers are thinking and feeling. When a leader shows empathy, it is confirming and validating for the follower. It makes the follower feel unique.

On 30th September 2005 in Delhi, Swamiji was examining arrangements for visitors at Akshardham. Swamiji arrived at Boot House and stared at the stairs nearby. Beyond this point, everyone must go barefooted to maintain holy dignity. Swamiji suggested to the management personnel to arrange for a carpet in summer so that no one's feet would be burnt due to the heated floor and the top of the stairs (Vicharan Report September 2005).

On 17th March 2009, Swamiji was in Sarangpur. I was protecting him with an umbrella from the sun rays. Some people were standing behind me. Swamiji stopped me, "Take care of the people behind. The umbrella may hurt someone." What could hurt others, it hurt him before (Vicharan Report March 2009)!

On 6th April 2008, Swamiji was in Sarangpur. The demolition of the Haveli was going on. 25 volunteers from Bhavnagar arrived for volunteering. Aruni Bhagat introduced them to Swamiji and then instructed those volunteers to start with the volunteering activities. Swamiji stopped Aruni Bhagat and asked, "Have they had their breakfast? First, arrange for the breakfast and then join them." Swamiji could understand others' needs over his (Vicharan Report April 2008).

Sterling K. Brown had said, "Empathy begins with understanding life from another person's perspective." On 1st March 2010, in Sarangpur an assembly was taking place in the afternoon. Swamiji arrived and immediately noticed that people were sitting out in the open under the harsh sun. Swamiji called Narayanmuni Swami and insisted arrangements be made to have a cover so no one would be affected by the hot conditions. For 5 to 7 minutes he was busy planning for his devotee's comfort. Another discussion was about their prasad (dinner). Every year during the Fuldol Festival, BAPS usually distributed packed food to devotees, but this time Swamiji wished to serve them with hot Khichdi. To serve hot and fresh Khichdi to more than 75,000 people was a challenge, but Swamiji determined to make it happen. He organized a team, and this wish to serve hot khichdi was a success (Vicharan Report March 2010).

On 10th November 2010, Swamiji was in Bochasan. Akhandmangal Swami arrived there with 300 youth during a tour from Valsad. The cooking department had some requirement for volunteering services. They were trying to engage these 300 youths for that. Swamiji once again showed his empathy and said, "They have been traveling for two days. They are tired, don't engage them there. Let them sleep so that they can continue with their journey ahead in the morning." Swamiji felt the feelings of others as his own (Vicharan Report November 2010).

Swamiji also knew about everyone's culture and their habits. On 20th September 2002, an American youth Thomas visited Sarangpur with Paramtattva Swami. He sat on the floor with the others. Swamiji asked Paramtattva Swami whether Thomas was comfortable sitting on floor or not. When Thomas indicated that he was comfortable, Swamiji was satisfied (Vicharan Report September 2002).

Zaleznik (1989) argued that businesspeople focused too much on process and structure, and not enough on ideas and emotions, and suggested that leaders should relate to followers in more empathetic and intuitive ways. Being empathetic to others is a smooth start to leadership path. Practicing it can gift us the sense of listening to others' hearts (Northouse, Leadership: Theory and Practice, 2016, p. 299).

On 26th July 2004, Swamiji was in Houston. At 7:30 in the morning, he was on his way to a pooja, traveling in a car. He saw Viveksagar Swamiji walking, stopped the car and offered him a ride (Vicharan Report July 2004).

On 2nd July 2004, Swamiji was in Orlando at a motel to conduct a training session. In his room, he noticed one of his sevaks trying to hang a wall clock. Swamiji said, "I am sure you are not making a new hole in the wall." The attendant replied, "No, I have not." Swamiji said, "We should not alter anything without the owner's permission" (Vicharan Report July 2004).

Aware of Others Likes and Dislikes

Swamiji is mindful of many of the devotees' likes and dislikes of food. When he learned that Ashokbhai Patel of Vadodara does not like tomatoes in his dal, he instructed his attendant sadhu to leave aside dal without any tomatoes. Whenever devotees are traveling with him, he takes care of their living accommodation, hot water, and meals. Swamiji knew that Natubhai from Nairobi could not have sweet items. When a dish was being prepared for him, Swamiji instructed, "He cannot eat sweet items, serve him chapattis instead." Natubhai was amazed and felt that even family members don't take such meticulous care (Sadhu V., 1997).

In 1988 Swamiji was in Bochum, Germany, at Dr. Arvindbhai's residence. A few devotees had driven 350 miles from Frankfurt just to have Swamiji's darshan. They had planned to leave a couple of hours later. Swamiji requested them to have some snacks. In the meantime, Swamiji also instructed the sadhus to pack some snacks for their long journey back. He also instructed them to include some sweet items and some spicy snacks as well. Swamiji's nature of caring for others' needs was born out of his love and concern for them (Sadhu V., 1997).

Reading Hearts

Malorie Blackman quotes, "Reading is an exercise in empathy." Yagnavallabh Swami had the same experience with Swamiji. He expressed it as, "In 1976, Swamiji celebrated Shri Hari Jayanti in Ahmedabad. It had been hardly six months since I had joined the BAPS as a youth. The next morning, Swamiji was offering his prayers (puja) in the presence of about 150 devotees. After the prayers, Swamiji was throwing the sanctified flowers offered in his prayers to the devotees. They felt blessed on receiving the flowers. I was sitting at the back that day. A thought arose in my mind, expecting a flower from Swamiji. But Swamiji did not even look at me. I consoled myself that I was still new to the Satsang and Swamiji doesn't even know me. Maybe, I would get that opportunity in the future. After prayers, Swamiji was proceeding to further programs. On the way, three youths, including myself, were standing. As Swamiji came nearer to us, he suddenly held my hand and gave me three rose flowers he had kept in his hand. Before I could realize that, he walked ahead." Yagnavallabh Swami was left stunned there thinking how Swamiji read his heart without any demand, words or expressions from him? (Swaminarayan Bliss, Nov-Dec, 2012).

A mother's heart can read her child without any words from him. Swamiji had that heart. On 11th June 2004, Swamiji was in Clarkston, Georgia, USA. A young man brought a six-month baby to Swamiji to be blessed. The baby was enjoying milk through a bottle. Suddenly, the man snatched the bottle from the baby, and it started coughing. He then attempted to place the bottle back in the baby's mouth, but the baby was still coughing. Swamiji stopped him from doing so and told him to wait until the baby was settled.

Sensitive to Other's Tears

Swamiji's compassion and empathy were fathomless. He could not bear tears in anyone's eyes. He felt the miseries of others. In 1987, Gujarat was in the grip of a severe drought. Cattle were dying all around. People were facing starvation. Swamiji instantly initiated a drought relief project. Around this time, Swamiji visited a cattle camp in Ratanpur, near Rajkot. There were about 5,000 drought-hit calves. Many of these young calves followed Swamiji wherever he walked around. The administrators informed Swamiji that for the past several days these calves have followed whoever came by since they have not had anything to eat. Swamiji was in tears and speechless on hearing it. He immediately went to Gondal and instructed Jnanprasad Swami, "I couldn't bear to see the poor, hungry calves running around behind me in Ratanpur. Please tell Yogiswarup Swami in Rajkot to send some truckloads of grass there right now." Every gesture of Swamiji reflected his deep concern for the difficulties people and animals were facing. Often, Swamiji sat alone lost in deep thought. And from this were born the exemplary BAPS Cattle Camps, where thousands of cattle were cared for. Once, Swamiji said, "I want to make arrangements to care for a lakh (100,000) cattle. Why can't we do that? Just look at their suffering. This is not a favor towards them, but a God-given opportunity to serve them. They have come to the feet of God." Due to Swamiji's compassion, management, decisiveness, and foresight, thousands of cattle were saved. The farmers declared, "Swamiji saved about our cattle. Who, except the most compassionate would do this?" (Swaminarayan Bliss Nov-Dec, 2015).

Swamiji also instructed the principals of the BAPS schools in Gondal and Bhadra not to take the school and boarding fees of students. For devotees and others affected by the drought, he provided buttermilk, sweet food items, and grains. After the drought, when the cattle were returned, he made arrangements for the cattle fodder to be sent along with their owners. During the next harvest, Swamiji refused donations of grains from those affected by the drought merely because they still had their debts to clear (Viveksagardas, 1997).

In 1989, Ajitbhai, a dedicated volunteer of village Kundi, Valsad district, passed away. At that time, Swamiji was in Dungri, a town in the same district. On hearing about Ajitbhai's demise, Swamiji said he wanted to go there. Acharya Swami explained, "His relatives are all very understanding, so there is no need to take the trouble of going there. And besides, we have to inform them in advance." However,

Swamiji wished to go, "He was a good volunteer. His village is on the way. We must go." Swamiji reached Ajitbhai's farm by dusk and met his father, Sukhabhai. His eldest son was away, but on hearing the sad news, he returned immediately. On seeing Swamiji, he was delighted with tears and said, "I knew you would come" (Viveksagardas, 1997).

Felt Other's Need and Helped

Tarana Burke says, "An exchange of empathy provides an entry point for a lot of people to see what healing feels like."

In August 1979, the Machchhu Dam in Morbi burst, resulting in widespread flooding. Swamiji was in Ahmedabad at the time. He was saddened on hearing news of the disaster. On All India Radio, Swamiji broadcast an appeal to BAPS volunteers everywhere to go to Morbi to help immediately. The response was swift and overwhelming. Under Swamiji's guidance, large-scale relief work was launched. Swamiji himself left Ahmedabad in the early morning to reach Morbi.

Speedily, Swamiji surveyed the situation by visiting the mud-filled homes and streets. His first decision was to set up a relief kitchen. He comforted the unfortunate victims. He prayed, "May all who have lost their lives be liberated and may the town quickly regain its vitality." Swamiji organized an efficient system to manage the relief work. Seeing Swamiji's rapid action in response to the flood, the Chief Minister of Gujarat, Babubhai Patel, and many others voiced, "With the help of Pramukh Swami Maharaj Morbi again became a habitable place. Pramukh Swami Maharaj's volunteers selflessly cleaned others' homes and raised their spirits."

While in Morbi, Swamiji pondered, "How will the Muslims of the town be able to celebrate their Eid festival tomorrow?" He called the Muslim leaders and invited all Muslims to dine at the BAPS relief kitchen. The next day, over 5,000 Muslims were treated to a celebratory meal including sweets and savory items. Swamiji's gesture touched everyone and demonstrated that he was a spiritual luminary beyond all differences (Swaminarayan Bliss Nov-Dec, 2015).

On 15th August 2016, in Sarangpur, the Prime Minister of India, Narendra Modi shared an empathetic experience, "In 2000, Pramukh Swami Maharaj performed the foundation-stone laying (Shilanyas) ceremony of Swaminarayan Akshardham in New Delhi. At that time, I felt how Swamiji would know about my presence while being engaged in a flurry of activities. There were many distinguished guests present in the Shilanyas ritual. I was there too because Pramukh Swami had said that I should participate in the rituals. Then, someone came hurriedly to me and gave me a few currency coins. He told me that Pramukh Swami had told him to give them to you because you would not have any coins to offer during the rituals. In reality, my pockets were empty. So, Pramukh Swami knew about it. Such was his empathy for me."

On another occasion, I was told to tell Pramukh Swami to have his meals because he had abstained from taking food altogether due to his illness at the age of 92. Since I was out, traveling far, I rang Swamiji and urged him, "Bapa, a son is telling you to start having your meals." Without any argument, he said, "Okay then, as you please." An hour later, I rang to check up, and I heard that Swamiji had taken his meal. Such close bonds I had experienced with him" (Swaminarayan Bliss September-October, 2016).

Awaking at Night

Empathy keeps a mother awake at nights. The same was true of Swamiji. He was attached to people, society, nation, and the world. The problem of others sometimes kept him awake praying for their problems.

In 1990, Swamiji visited England. One night, at about 2:30 a.m., Swamiji's attendant sadhu suddenly woke up. He saw Swamiji sitting up on his bed. A closer look revealed that Swamiji had folded his hands and closed his eyes in prayer. For half-an-hour, the attendant sadhu observed Swamiji.

When Swamiji opened eyes, the sadhu asked, "What were you praying for?"

Swamiji replied, "There is a severe drought in India and people are struggling without water. I was praying for the rains so that all people and animals have enough water to strive."

The sadhu enquired further, "How often have you prayed for this?" But Swamiji remained silent. The attendant politely and repeatedly asked the question. Eventually, Swamiji revealed, "Many times I pray at night. During the day many people present their questions and problems to me, so I pray for them."

Empathy is like an iceberg. One can express it 10% through words and helping actions. 90% of it is silent and unseen deep into the heart. No one knew till this day that Swamiji often pray at night for them. The attendant sadhu was deeply touched by Swamiji's night-time prayers for others (Swaminarayan Bliss Nov-Dec, 2015).

Empathy Grows a Community

People wonder how Swamiji could build a volunteer force of 75,000, initiated 1000 youths to sacrifice their lives in service of humanity for a lifetime? How could he make a change and transform the lives of more than one million people? How could he build a moral and spiritual community at large?

> *"Empathy is the starting point for creating a community and taking action. It's the impetus for creating change."* - Max Carver

Yes, empathy can add even prejudiced people to a leader's community. Einstein said, "It is harder to break prejudice than an atom." But a leader cracks it through empathy and the community grows eventually. On 9th January 2010, Swamiji was staying at Prayaswinbhai's bungalow. He appointed one of his trusted executive Niranjanbhai Maharana to care for Swamiji's necessities. Somehow, he had some prejudice for sadhus before. But Swamiji's presence and empathy turned his attitude, and Niranjan Maharana became Swamiji's great fan. The dislikes at the beginning dissolved. He became so involved serving Swamiji that his wife suspected, "I am afraid you will become a monk." Niranjan said, "Maybe even this may happen. So, please inform your father living in Bihar. I insist to you as well, why don't you come for Swamiji's darshan and listen to his discourses." Stephen Covey remarks, "When you show deep empathy towards others, their defensive energy goes down, and positive energy replaces it." Swamiji's selfless empathy converted Narendra Maharana's negative energy to positive energy.

Pramukh Swami Maharaj founded the community through his empathy. He treated the community by understanding their feelings. Though he was an iconic personality, he always kept himself grounded with people, and this allowed him to be empathetic toward their hardships.

He became their path, showing the way.

He became their compass, showing the direction.

He became their mother, comforting them on their long journey.

> *"Leadership is about empathy. It is about having the ability to relate to and connect with people for the purpose of inspiring and empowering their lives."*
>
> ~ Oprah Winfrey ~

20. Training

"Good teachers know how to bring out the best in students."
~ Charles Kuralt ~

Training followers is like a job of a sculptor. He has a tool in his hand, and he carves a beautiful piece out of it with gentle care and patience. A leader knows it takes time and patience to turn a layperson into a skilled worker. Many leadership theories present different approaches to nourishing the skills of subordinates.

The Behavior Approach presents a leadership grid and remarks on concern for people over a task. The Situational Approach developed by Blanchard is the most frequently used approach for training leaders within organizations. Today, 400 out of the fortune 500 companies use the situational factor to train their managers and leaders. It requires that a leader adapt different styles in different situations to meet the demands and needs of the followers. The Situational Approach suggest directive and supportive dimensions apply in different situations. In Directive Behavior, a leader gives directions, establishes goals and methods, sets timeline, defines roles and shows how to achieve the goal. It's a one-way communication on what to do, how, and who is responsible for that. A Supportive Behavior leader helps followers personally get their job done and empower them to ask for input, solving problems, praising, sharing information, and listening. A leader should be able to identify with a follower or situation what dimension he needs to adapt at that moment. Based on requirements and the combination of supportive and directive behaviors, they produce four kinds of styles: Directing (S1), Coaching(S2), Supportive (S3) and, Delegating (S4).

If we think of a family, we may find that parents without learning Situational Leadership are very effectively living it in their daily routines with their children. Initially, a child doesn't know how to eat, how to walk or how to behave with certain relatives. The parents support the child. Once a child learns the behaviors, they become directive as to what to eat, and when to eat. Now the parents focus their attention to train their child in sports, language and other necessary activities. We can observe supportive and directive, sometimes both the behaviors simultaneously in parents when they deal with different situations and activities. It's surprising how they know and master it? Without any training in Situational Approach, they practice it very effectively. The root cause behind it is – they have a deep feeling within them, 'It is my child, it belongs to my family.' It's a sense of familyhood. Leaders have these same feelings – for larger groups. Leaders do not spend time analyzing the situation and deciding which style they need to adapt to a particular situation? The inspiration sprouts from within what the followers need and how one should act? Does a mother spend time thinking, "Oh, my son is ill, he is sick in bed. What style should I adopt in this situation?" She doesn't think much. Instead, she supports her son to get well soon and directs him to take his medicines on time, and rest well for a quick recovery.

Pramukh Swamiji thought the whole world as one family. He could understand the follower's needs very quickly and adapted to different styles as per the situation.

Directive Style

It is a high directive-low supportive style, which is also called a Directing Style. In this approach, the leader focuses on communication on goal achievement and spends less time using supportive behaviors. Using this style, a leader gives instructions about what and how goals are to be achieved by the followers and then supervises them carefully.

Swamiji exhibited all the characteristics of a perfect directive behavior. One of his best directive behaviors was witnessed when there was an earthquake in Gujarat. It was 26th January 2001. At 8.46 a.m. a devastating earthquake rattled Gujarat. It measured 7.6 on the Richter Scale, demolishing buildings, infrastructure and killing thousands. The most affected area was Bhuj and its surrounding towns and villages.

That morning, Swamiji was in Bochasan 418.8 km away from Bhuj. Swamiji gave immediate directions to sadhus and volunteers to start relief work. Government officials were amazed that by noon, BAPS was serving a fresh meal to the survivors. The next day, more than 40,000 people were fed warm and nutritious meals, and this went on for a few more days. Swamiji ensured that the menu changed everyday, so that people could enjoy variety. Attending to the minutest of details, Swamiji called Vedagna Swami, the Kothari in Bochasan, regarding the grains being sent to

Bhuj, "The grains that are being ground for the relief kitchens have to be of the best quality. Make sure they are cleaned and sifted for small stones." Swamiji visited the kitchen in Atladra where food packets for distribution were being prepared. After inspection, he suggested that two green pickled chilies be included in each packet, explaining, "People from the Kutch region enjoy spicy food. Also, they will taste good with the sweets." Swamiji coordinated the Sanstha's earthquake relief work, often staying up till well past midnight to contact people in India and abroad to make the necessary arrangements.

"If evolution really works, how come mothers only have two hands?"
~ Milton Berle ~

Though having two hands, Swamiji inspired and directed thousands of hands to reach out to the victims of the earthquake. People felt Swamiji caring for them through thousands of hands and heart of a mother. One-night, Swamiji was worried for the children's schooling and initiated tin halls to start their education with immediate effect. He joined those volunteers who were teachers by profession, to teach so that the children's education didn't suffer. After a few days, he was worried about the victim's nails and sent nail cutters for them. He was aware that some wealthy families were too shy to stand in queues and did not want to come to the relief camp for meals. Swamiji arranged to serve 700 tiffins to their homes. Before the victims felt the need, Swamiji served it! Swamiji inquired why so many people had fractures after the earthquake? He was told that they did not have sufficient shoes. On the same day, he arranged for the shoes to be delivered through volunteers. More than 500 villages were provided with aid, and 15 villages and colonies were reconstructed. Swamiji personally walked through the rubble-strewn streets of the earthquake-devastated villages in Kutch, showering his grace and compassion to the survivors. He blessed the injured and traumatized victims to lessen their pain and sorrow.

Coaching Style

In this approach, the leader focuses communication on both achieving goals and meeting the followers' socio-emotional needs. The coaching style requires that the leader involve himself or herself with followers by giving encouragement and soliciting follower input.

Yagyapurush Smriti Mandir was under construction at Sarangpur. The inauguration was planned for 1981. The contractor informed Swamiji that due to a shortage of labor, there would be a delay. The necessary stones were placed at a distance. Swamiji said, "I will come there in the evening to start volunteering." He came and started lifting the stones. Some devotees were standing at a distance. Swamiji called everyone around and motivated them through his action.

Pramukh Swami Maharaj was not concerned for task or people, but his concern was developing people at all aspects whether it was an important task to welcome Prime Minister or cleaning the room. On 18th December 2004, in Navsari, Swamiji arrived at the newly built accommodation buildings for devotees. There he insisted, "The toilet-bathrooms should always remain clean from every corner. Have you seen the airports or the motels? How clean are they? We should have similar standards. If you cannot maintain, hire labor, but it should be cleaned every day. If you do not pay attention to all these things, then people will devalue us. So, if you have to hire labor, hire them, but it must be cleaned every day."

"A coach is someone who can give correction without causing resentment."
~ John Wooden ~

In Mumbai, 1966, two senior devotees were in an important meeting with Yogiji Maharaj and Pramukh Swami. During the meeting, Haribhushan Swami took in some fruits and milk as refreshments for the guests. In his haste, some of the milk spilled into one of the saucers. Pramukh Swami noted this but remained silent. After the meeting, Swamiji called Haribhushan Swami aside. Without appearing domineering in any way whatsoever, he gently corrected, "Haribhushan, remember one thing; never fill a glass of milk or water up to the brim. It shouldn't spill over into the saucers. If necessary, pour a little less into the glass so that not even a drop overflows."
Swamiji goes into great detail to explain to the sadhus the importance of mastering a simple task. Only those who have the patience to do simple things perfectly, ever acquire the skill to do difficult things easily. Haribhushan Swami later noted, 'This small but important lesson of etiquette taught by Swamiji proved to be helpful to me on many occasions' (The Current Spiritual Guru Pramukh Swami Maharaj, n.d.).

"A life coach does for the rest of your life what a personal trainer does for your health and fitness."
~ Elaine Macdonald ~

Most people refer to training in reference to some task or talent. But socioemotional training is more important than this. Swamiji did it nicely. On 8th May 2005 in Ahmedabad, Purushottamcharan Swami informed Swamiji regarding the water shortage in Gondal and the trouble faced by the temple. He said, "We have sought and lawfully got a separate line." Swamiji immediately responded saying, "If you do for your own only, then others will throw you away. Do for all and ours will also be taken care of. Swamiji imparted wonderful core values."

On 2nd February 2012, Swamiji called the head cook and blessing him said, 'That is how you keep feeding everyone with love. Peacefully without losing patience, do the work with the volunteers lovingly, so that everyone is happy and serve with zeal."

On 11th July 2006 in Bochasan, there was a discussion about a 3-day discourse program. Narayanmuni Swami said, "Mahant Swamiji will talk on how others can understand me?" Swamiji then said, "The essence is one should understand others. If we understand others, people will understand us." Swamiji summarized the philosophy of human relationship in few words.

On 11th March 2009 in Sarangpur, a senior volunteer from abroad met Swamiji and said, "I don't want to continue with volunteering service and want to quit now." Swamiji knew about his dominating and outspoken nature. He also knew his dedication and tremendous effort he had put in. Swamiji turned around the situation to a positive one within a few minutes. He gave this senior volunteer some important advice. Swamiji said to him, "You are blessed. You've done good work and doing well. Everyone knows all that. Your opponents also know, but discrimination takes place due to attitude. Therefore, there is opposition. And once you face the opposition, you do not have to look right or wrong. So always move ahead with advice from everyone. Cooperate everywhere. If you do this in a good way, you will get the job done. The cause of opposition is our attitude and nature. If you say something adverse, then people's ego will be hurt. We should talk softly. If you listen twice to them, they will be satisfied, because when we work with people, everyone has a different nature. We should not expect all to follow our interests. If we work with humility, then everyone will become positive. If someone comes up with a complaint, rather than refusing to say, 'Ok, we will look into it, think about it.' If there is politeness in speech, half the work is done."

And those who oppose, forget about all the opposition, behave nicely with them, seek their advice and they will start supporting you. So, if someone has done anything do not keep any grudge against them. Keeping a grudge does not work. And be patient in meetings. You should listen at least 50%, and then others will also listen to you. Your good conduct can resolve disputes. Learn to compromise. By seeking someone's advice, does not demean us. Instead, it improves our esteem. So, keep this in mind."

Swamiji presented this socialism for the understanding of all.

Supportive Style

The Supportive Style includes listening, praising, asking for input and giving feedback. We can see all these qualities in Swamiji during an event as described by Narayanmuni Swami. "In 1983, Swamiji suffered a heart attack. So, there was no arrangement to meet him in person after the assembly." That year on the occasion of Guru Punam, I went to Swamiji and said, "After you finish your blessing discourse, you will be going to your accommodation site." Swamiji expressed his desire to meet in person to all the devotees. I reminded him about his delicate health. But he insisted on staying there. So, I explained the reality to him, "It's a huge crowd. We have not made any arrangement so that they can queue up and meet you. Your speech will begin in a while. So, it is not possible to make any arrangement now."

Hearing this, Swamiji said, "Why can't it be done? See, one volunteer will take care of 50 devotees. But he should be cautious. He should keep an eye on all. If someone stands up in the middle, he will have to tell them to sit down."

I replied, "The volunteers you talk about cannot be found at this late hour. The assembly hall is packed to capacity. So, it is not possible."

Then, Swamiji said encouragingly, "You are afraid without any reason. If you wish it, you can do everything."

I said, "That is all right, but how is it possible at this hour?"

Swamiji said, "Try it at least."

I said, "I will try since you want me to, but it is not likely to succeed."

As this talk ended, the previous program ended, and it was time for Swamiji's speech. After announcing of Swamiji's blessings, I went at the back of the assembly hall. Arunbhai was in charge of the assembly arrangements, so I told him what was on Swamiji's mind. He said, "It will be done."

He at once called some selected volunteers and instructed them about the arrangement. After Swamiji's blessings, the volunteers positioned themselves in the middle of the assembly hall. The arrangement for individual darshan was made without the need for pushing or hurrying the devotees as they passed before Swamiji. For years, we had been searching for a solution to avoid pushing the devotees who wished for personal darshan; Swamiji provided us with the solution during a casual discussion. At last, when Swamiji was descending from the stage, he told me, "Your planning was good. Thank you. It was Swamiji's idea, and he gave credit to me." Here Swamiji listened to the problem, gave his feedback, suggested a working solution and also praised for its success.

Delegating Style

Here the leader lessens involvement in planning, control of details, and goal clarification. After the group agrees on what it is to do, this style lets followers take responsibility for getting the job done the way they see fit. The leader gives control to followers and refrains from intervening with additional social support.

Pramukh Swamiji trained the team members to the extent that the team trained many other members to the same high professional level. At BAPS, 2-3 big festival events in a month were common. Those events brought together, 50,000 to 100,000 devotees. One of the major departments was the kitchen which had the task of feeding all the devotees in one sitting. The head of the department Brahmtirth Swami went to Swamiji and requested he be provided with skilled volunteers. Swamiji said, "Now you should train the volunteers as you are trained." Brahmtirth Swami trained other sadhus. A few years later, there was another line of skilled volunteers ready for kitchen duties without any directive from Swamiji. This happened to all the departments like parking, stage, decoration, accommodation, waterworks, press & media, cultural department, and many others. Swamiji trained the first line of sadhus, and then they trained in succession.

> *"True leaders don't create followers...they create more leaders!"*
>
> *~ J Sakiya Sandifer ~*

21. Field Specific Traits

"A leader is someone who helps improve the lives of other people or improve the system they live under."
~ Sam Houston ~

There is a discussion at the start of the book about a leader's personal traits and field-specific traits. The different fields of leadership demand different traits. A political field leader might not have business field traits. A business field leader might not have social servant traits; a conceptual leader might not have political or business field traits. But all leaders, irrespective of their fields must have good character, politeness, goal/vision, conceptual, motivating, patience, and problem-solving. Apart from these other leadership skills are field-specific.

A youngster came to Swamiji and said, "My father was in the military for several years. Now he wants to start a business. Swamiji said, "It's tough now. In business, ones need to be very polite, flexible and ready to compromise. His nature might be a little arrogant and stiff due to his services in the military for a long period."

Different fields demand different skill sets. Some skills essential for a field might be controversial in another field. A military leader need not be as empathetic, but a person in the medical field (like a clinic or a hospital) need to be empathetic. A medical practitioner needs to give immediate attention to scratches and cuts, but a military leader can ignore minor injuries on the battlefield. He needs to encourage his comrades to continue to combat despite a bullet passing through his palm. Here, courage is more important over empathy.

Some characteristics as we think essential for a leader are not required at all for a specific field. Team management seems to be an essential characteristic for a leader, but there are so many leaders like Mother Teresa who didn't require it. It is essential for Jeff Bezos or Abraham Lincoln. Some conceptual leaders may or may not require team management. Field-specific characteristic varies according to the field, but the basic personal leadership traits discussed in chapter five are constant. Let's test it with conceptual leaders.

Conceptual Leader

Einstein was a conceptual leader. A conceptual leader launches a concept. Sometimes people don't understand those principle/concept when a leader is alive. After some decades or centuries, people feel the necessity or truth and, they follow it. In these cases, the leader is not present physically, but his concept is leading. We can understand it through other examples. Gandhiji gave us the concept of non-violence; Martin Luther King Jr. didn't meet Gandhiji even once. He learned the concept and led a movement. Nelson Mandela was in jail for 28 years. He couldn't form the team for the movement in jail. He was not present among the followers though he was leading the people through his concept. To summarize, I can say a conceptual leader may or may not form a team himself.

Service Oriented Fields:

Some of the fields are service oriented like the medical, retail business, social services, etc. In these fields, the leader needs more of a servant leadership trait. Like a computer selling company, it requires to be more customer service focused than to focus specifically on its employee's physical strength. But a soccer leader needs to concentrate more on the physical, mental, and soccer skills of their team members and has far more limited focus on customer service.

Now let's discuss some field-specific traits. There might be some more traits on a specific field than listed here. Still, some common among them are as follows (1) Service Orientation (2) Knowledge / Technical Skills (3) Team Management (4) Media Control (5) Policy and (6) Infrastructure.

Knowledge/Technical Skills:

It helps a leader to lead effectively if he has knowledge of his field. It's a field-specific trait. It is specific to the fields and differs accordingly. A soccer or basketball coach must possess good knowledge of the game to lead a team. While a Business CEO need not possess knowledge of all the departments or manufacturing process of all the products. As the Skills Approach suggests, at top management level; human skills and conceptual skills are mandatory and technical skill is optional. Therefore, knowledge is a field-specific trait.

Team Management

Most fields demand a team. There are only a few fields like conceptual or intellect as discussed earlier which don't require a team. A leader should be able to build an efficient team, align it to its goal, able to establish unity among team members, win team member's trust and their will to sacrifice for the leader. Pramukh Swami Maharaj could build a tremendous team. He could build a dedicated team to work for him for zero wages, 14 to 18 hours a day without any holiday or Sunday for a lifetime. There are 1000 such team members still working for him. Another 20, 000 volunteers are working for him after their day to day professions for 3 to 10 hours a day. Swamiji could win their trust in him to the extent that they wouldn't cross his words and follow him with faith and devotion. These volunteers didn't suspect Swamiji's decisions and followed those decisions sincerely as directed. Swamiji could build the team through his familyhood, care, empathy, training, emotional support, counseling, responsibility, and sacrifice; previously been discussed in detail earlier.

Media

This is also an important field specific trait. Some leadership fields may require this, and some may not. This is an era of social media. A leader must understand the impact of media. Use of social media effectively can grow an organization to unbelievable heights. If a leader is not aware, it can cause irreparable loss to the organization. When there was a terrorist attack on Akshardham, Swamiji first published the appeal for peace in the media. If it had not been done timely, it could have cost thousands of lives and a permanent repute loss, and adverse consequences to the organization. A sadhu Parmatma Swami was shot dead late at night. Swamiji decided not to disclose this news to the media and declared it later when everything settled. If he had not been prompt in handling this sensitive issue, there would have been other repercussions in the future. Today, a leader must be cautious when it comes to the media. A rumor, misquotes, words said in anger, can have devastating results.

During a course on 'Leadership Perspective' from Harvard, they assigned a case study to us regarding servant leadership. A storm hit the east coast and passengers of nine flights were stranded on the runway of JFK airport, New York. The JetBlue airlines could not take the necessary measures and paid $30 million to customers. The root cause was they could not handle the media as it should be. The airlines image was ruined overnight. At last Neeleman (CEO, JetBlue) had to resign. If he could manage the media, the loss could have been prevented, and the company's image could have been saved. Pramukh Swamiji established an intelligent public relations department where news disclosure would take place at the right time.

Policy/Principles

Complete Leadership

A leader must define the principles of the organization and stick to them. It is different from a goal. It's a list of policies or principles a leader set out to help followers decide what to do and what not to do in any circumstances. It is more related to ethical decisions and sets the boundary of an organization and members for their behavior and actions.

On 9th January 2001, Swamiji was in Bochasan. Swamiji's birthday celebration was over in Anand. Swamiji called Sarvamangal Swamiji and said, "I have received a letter from a devotee. He has mentioned that advertising for tobacco products and a poultry farm are being printed on our souvenirs. Please take care of it. For the things we deny people, how is it we advertise for it? Even if we are offered millions of rupees, we should not entertain it at any cost. I want all the admin people to remember this forever."

A man came to Swamiji and said, "I want to donate a big amount to the organization." Swamiji knew about his business malpractice and said to him, "First be honest in your business practice. We don't need your donation. Be a person of moral and spiritual values first."

On another occasion, Swamiji was conducting an earthquake relief project. An organization from abroad offered a handsome amount of donation for this project. Swamiji asked, "How did they raise this amount?" Later he found out the money was raised out of gambling. Swamiji politely declined the donation.

Once a person wrote against Swamiji, his spiritual activities and organization in newspapers. Without thinking, many core team members decided to respond through newspapers. They drafted the content to be released to the media. When they came to show it to Swamiji, he said, "It's not our policy. Shastriji Maharaj never replied to anyone's allegations. Our policy is to tolerate, we never compliment others, criticize or reply to anyone's allegations."

An organization was opposing Swamiji for years. One day an advocate met Swamiji with a confidential file with him. The file was full of strong evidence of malpractices from that organization. The advocate said, "I am giving you this file. You can present it to the government and ruin them." Swamiji said, "Destroy these pieces of evidence. It's not our policy to degrade anyone, even our enemy. Our policy is to think good of all and do good to all."

On 27th August 2004 in London, Swamiji met a volunteer. He was active in local politics. The party invited him to participate in the next elections. He said to Swamiji, "Please inspire some devotees to participate in the elections." Swamiji said, "We are a religious organization, and we do not encourage anyone for politics. During elections, we bless every candidate. Politics is not our principle, so we cannot do anything like that here. We bless all who come here."

On 26th November 2000 in Mumbai, Swamiji's symbolic 80th birth celebration was over. An eye hospital with extensive facilities was aided with 100% free services.

Dr. Kiran Doshi remarked, "You pleased Mumbai by making 100% free treatment in the Eye Hospital." Swamiji commented, "But keep in mind to treat at par all patients rich, poor or needy. Do not discriminate in treating the poor." Swamiji had a policy - treat every individual without any discrimination of caste, religion, country, gender or race either rich or poor.

On 25th August 2005 in Atladra, Swamiji's car met an accident and was damaged. The driver brought the car back after the repairs and mentioned that as the insurance policy had matured, there was no expense required to be paid for the car repairs and the insurance company had taken care of the expenses." Swamiji said, "We did pay for the insurance for it to mature in the first place." Swamiji felt there was no such thing as I paid or he paid. Any loss to anyone else is a loss to us. It was his extended familyhood to shelter the entire world under one roof.

The above are policy related decisions made by Swamiji, of a socio-spiritual organization. Other fields might have some different policy & principles with some commonality within this set.

As we understand it, the term 'Leader' is normally associated with someone leading a huge group for an extraordinary cause. But we need to change this perspective. A simple scenario is 'The leader leads a group.' The group need not be large always. The group may be of a single person – leading himself, a family, two persons, few persons and up to millions and billions of people. The 'Complete Leadership' definition applies to any group of any size ranging from a person or family up to the nation and the world. It also implies that a group can have a leader and sub-leaders. Sub-leaders may lead sub-groups, and the leader leads all of them towards a common good cause and goal/vision.

"Leadership knows: it does not believe."

~ Lamine Pearlheart ~

22. Infrastructure

"Be so good they can't ignore you."
~ Steve Martin ~

There is a lot of talk on leadership, and there are many best-selling books available. That is the theoretical part. But the major problem is of practical implementation - how to learn those habits, how to turn our attitudes? What to do? How to accomplish it? Where to learn? Swamiji talked less and did most by providing a one-stop solution to develop all aspects of life and built an infrastructure for that.

Pramukh Swami Maharaj established the infrastructure for personal, intellectual, professional, emotional, social, moral and spiritual development. Such a state-of-the-art infrastructure to develop all aspects is nowhere to be found. Most organizations or institutions provide infrastructure to develop only personal, professional & intellectual aspects of a person. Even, most countries lack this infrastructure. Parents, educational institutions, NGOs, commercial organizations and government don't have a capable system to deal with moral & social problems.

To develop the moral and spiritual aspects, Swamiji trained a team of 1000 sadhus and 65,000 volunteers. He built more than 1100 mandirs and cultural centers. To provide moral & spiritual content, he developed a systematic infrastructure that spreads literature. It encompasses a state-of-the-art publishing press, chain of the bookstore, several monthly magazines, books, and organized events. Swamiji started weekly assemblies to nurture these aspects further.

In 1986, a delegation of senior sadhus visited the Mercedes manufacturing plant. The administrator said, "We have added 100 corrections this year to avoid accidents." A sadhu asked, "Who does the accident? Car or humans?" The question puzzled him, and he kept quiet. The sadhu said, "It's a human, We need more corrections there." If someone is drunk and driving the car, any car with the latest corrections and technology won't work."

Many organizations are trying to find a cure and spending billions of dollars behind it. But no one has thought to repair human instinct and discipline. Swamiji's guidance, strategy, and infrastructure helped thousands of people learn self-control. Below are some details provided about the infrastructure Swamiji established for complete development.

As we build a hospital, we require doctors to cure patients. To train the doctors, one requires training institutes. Swamiji built mandirs and training centers to train sadhus and volunteers to cure human nature and help them with learn self-control. Swamiji built a training center for monks and volunteers at Sarangpur. It's a one-of-a-kind training center in the world which puts so much focus on human

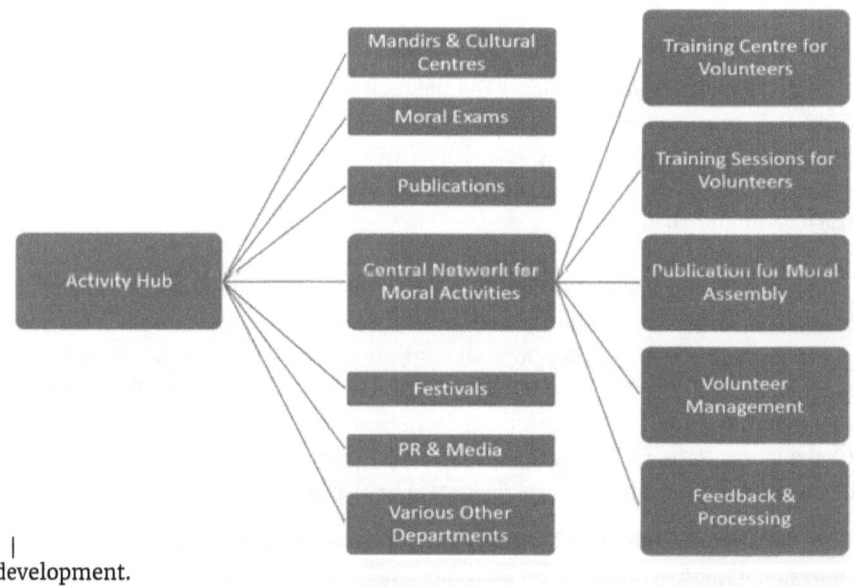

development.

The Activity Hub is the administration center to manage numerous activities for the overall development of people. At present, 1200 mandirs and cultural centers are operating under its guidance. Mandirs and cultural centers are the subunits of infrastructure that manages all the activities and moral assemblies at a local level.

There is a team of sadhus and volunteers who publish books, various monthly magazines with a subscriber base of 120,000. Followers receive moral stories, an article on Mahant Swami Maharaj – inspiring incidents from his life to learn and practice in daily life. The magazines are unique as they cater to different groups. For kids, the magazine content is specific to their needs, for women, the content is geared towards their needs and development.

The activity hub also conducts moral exams twice a year. Around 40,000 followers participate in the exam. They have to read moral value books, and upon passing the exam, they receive certificates. These exams strengthen moral and spiritual values & discipline in devotees. It also creates awareness of the BAPS organization and conveys the vision to the devotees.

The central network for moral development is unique. It manages 65,000 volunteers, produces new volunteers through 6-month training centers, conducts yearly training sessions to sharpen their skill sets. It is responsible for providing publication to sadhus & volunteers for running moral assemblies. It prepares the agenda and program for various moral/spiritual assemblies. Sadhus and volunteers run moral assemblies according to the prescribed literature and program. They send the program feedback through various feedback forms. The central office keeps records of registration and various details of each assembly. At present, over 20,000 weekly, biweekly or monthly assemblies are operated and managed successfully under it in India and throughout the world. There are three other similar wings for the development of elders, children, youth and women. The central department maintains uniformity of programs and training for all.

Mega festivals unite the follower's community. There are one or two mega festivals each year. It's a one to ten days festival and requires about 12,000 volunteers to manage for 1.5 million visitors. The most remarkable fact is, there is almost zero budget. People donate the goods, grains, and their volunteer services to make it a success. Volunteers cook and serve fresh meals to 50,000 – 200,000 people every day. The festival operates on 300 to 500 acres of land. There is a giant 500 x 200 feet stage to host the mega-events; various inspirational shows on moral, social, personal & spiritual values; thematic gardens; bookstores; food stalls and many more. More than 38 departments act to manage parking, unrestricted public flow, decoration, stage events, kitchen, cultural programs, etc. The stage programs are very inspirational and full of varieties. On the main festival day, more than 200,000 people gather to learn lessons for life. Millions of other watches it live on TV channels. The vision & values of organization and leader are shared to followers. It has a significant impact on the lives of the followers and the general public. Thousands of people give up addictions, many give up bad habits and take vows for their personal development. Festivals play a significant role in the development of people at large.

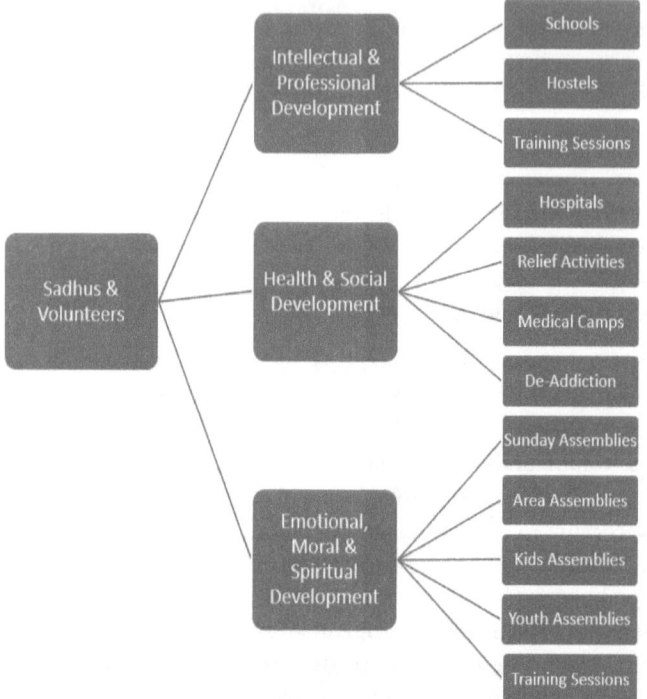

In the previous section, we saw the administration part of the infrastructure. Here we can view the development part of a person. Sadhus and volunteers run different activities to develop all the aspects of an individual. They run schools, hostels and conduct various training sessions to develop the intellectual and professional faces. Here the primary difference is - along with the intellectual part, they are taught moral and spiritual lessons in parallel. Every day there is a special assembly and activity for this. Health & social development is carried out through free medical camps, yoga camps, blood donation camps, yoga sessions, and de-addiction camps. Some valuable publications are published for health awareness. Swamiji started a herbal care unit to produce 100% pure herbal medicines for followers. These units are not established for profit-making, but to serve the people with devotion.

The emotional, moral and spiritual aspect is developed through daily, weekly or monthly assemblies. The content is based on current personal, occupational, social, family and national or international problems. These moral assemblies are the backbone of other development aspects. Here people learn moral and spiritual values through different audio-visual media and discourses. They listen to moral incidents from past and present. It inspires them to put it in practice. There are several projects to help them put it in practice. It's a theory and practical class to implement the values for life in practice effectively. The community factor also helps with it. As earlier discussed, the assembly programs are different for different age groups, keeping in mind their development phase and requirements.

Here we look at a glance some unusual incidents and facts. The details reveal why there is a necessity for the emotional, moral and spiritual development of children & youth.

(1) Kayla Rolland, a six-year-old girl was murdered on February 29, 2000. Rolland was shot and killed by her classmate Dedrick Owens, also 6-years-old, at Buell Elementary School in the Beecher Community School District (Shooting of Kayla Rolland, n.d.).

(2) Claverie, 21, asked his father Weber to leave, the police said. When his father refused, Claverie got a pistol and shot his father four to six times, killing him. Police said Weber had been drinking before he arrived and the two got into an argument, Claverie got excited and shot his father dead. (Son charged with murder in shooting death of father at southwest Houston apartment, 2018).

(3) Dr. Hollis S. Ingraham, New York Health Commissioner, warned at a World Conference in New York, "Cigarettes are more lethal for Americans than all the bullets, germs and viruses combined!"

(4) In the United States, 7.6% (1.1 million) of high school students smoke, every year 4,80,000 people die of smoke, 16 million suffering smoking-caused illness, Annual health care expenditure caused by smoking is $170 Billion (The Toll of Tobacco in the United States, n.d.).

(5) According to the World Health Organization (WHO), tobacco caused **100 million** deaths in the 20th century. Those estimates include military and civilian deaths (cigarettes or war which is the biggest killer, n.d.).

(6) BALTIMORE (WBAL/CNN) - A high school student assaulted a Baltimore high school teacher in class Wednesday. "Ensuring a safe teaching and learning environment for our students and staff is paramount to city schools," city school officials said in a statement. "Upon reviewing the incident, school administrators will apply disciplinary action in accordance with Baltimore City Public Schools' code of conduct" (High school student punches veteran teacher in face, n.d.).

(7) A 17-year-old student armed with a shotgun and pistol has opened fire in a Texas high school, killing nine fellow students and a teacher, authorities say, in an attack similar to the massacre at a Florida high school in February (Texas School Shooting Leaves 10 People Dead, 2018).

There are many more alarming incidents in regard to lower moral and spiritual values. Pramukh Swami Maharaj started teaching children about moral and spiritual values over 50 years ago. Today, the children's emotional, social, moral and spiritual development aspect is well established through a well-thought infrastructure. The image below illustrates it.

Bal Prakash Magazine

The 'Bal Prakash' is a magazine for children. It is published every month and contains everything children require to develop every aspect of their life.

Parents

Parents play a significant role in children's development. Children imitate values and behavior of their parents. Swamiji knew it. He built the infrastructure to develop them as well.

Children Assembly

Children assemblies are customized to suit children and their mindset. It contains a variety of programs where they can learn values while playing games and participating in activities.

Sadhus & Volunteers

Sadhus and volunteers interact with each child, understand them, counsel them, help them improve their habits, character, and behavior.

Prayers, Seva, De-Addiction

At BAPS, many children learn to pray daily in the morning. They don't sip a drop of water before prayers. They learn to serve their parents and help them give up smoking or alcohol.

Study Guidance

BAPS also organizes special classes and guidance seminars where renowned teachers and professionals explore the study techniques and guidance for children and youth.

Social Services Projects

Daily Moral Activities

During vacations, instead of sitting idle and not being purposeful, children join various projects to serve society. They go to hospitals to meet and pray for patients and join the de-addiction drive to create an addiction-free society. They are asked to perform several moral activities like respect parent, teachers, guests, and volunteering and elders. Eventually, it turns into good habits. Yearly Training Seminars (Shivirs) add value, and it is entrenched in the minds of children that to serve others is a selfless act and will help them in many areas of their lives when they grow up.

A similar infrastructure is run for youths and elderly followers with a few changes. Youth activities are designed with specific considerations. There are packed with professional development, personality development along with other aspects. They receive expert guidance for their career from experienced professionals. They take an active part in social services during their vacation or after office hours. 'Sunday for Swamiji' is a slogan where youth gather at cultural centers on Sundays. They spend the whole day there listening to discourses; serving others by cleaning the ground and campus, preparing food, cleaning utensils, and many other activities. They also develop their cultural part by participating in folk dance, moral drama, acting, mono-acting, reciting, debates, speech, etc. The center also organizes zonal tournaments such as cricket, football, badminton, table tennis, and many other games and events to create balance. They learn moral and spiritual lessons here – honesty, self-restraint, fasting, offering daily prayers, drug & tobacco-free life, respect parents and obey them, celibacy till marriage, etc.

For the elders, the main focus is on social, moral and spiritual development. This is offered through weekly assemblies on Sundays or at cultural centers on weekdays in the evening. If possible, the elderly can also do 'Gharsabha.' Gharsabha is a novel concept developed by Swamiji. Here, the family members get together. They recite holy name, sing hymns, read scriptures and moral books. Gharsabha allows for the family members to get closer. Thousands of families who started practicing this concept, are of the opinion that their family conflicts have resolved, and it brought them peace of mind.

> *"Be the start of something that is good, revolutionary and powerful. Everything after that is a bonus."*
>
> *~ Carlos Wallace ~*

23. Outcome – Development of People

"Don't tell people how to do things, tell them what to do and let them surprise you with their results."
~ George Patton ~

Development of people is similar to the process of building a house. First, we have to clean the shrubs and flatten the uneven land to prepare it to lay the foundation. Then a hole has to be dug up to fill in the foundation before the construction work begins. The bricks are bonded together using high-quality cement. Once the house is complete, it is painted, and the electricity and water connections are added. The house is then furnished and decorated. Some landscaping and gardening work is carried out. After a lengthy process, the house is now ready for us to move in. We enjoy living in it. We can't miss any aspect of the building process to live comfortably in the

home. If there was no foundation, there would be no house, to begin with. If there no water or electricity, you would not be living there. Decorating the home makes it livable, and the greenery adds peace of mind.

Developing people is a process just like building a house. If we miss certain aspects, it's incomplete and causes discomforts and problems. There are seven aspects to develop a person to its full extent. (1) Moral Development (2) Professional Development (3) Personal Development (4) Emotional Development (5) Social Development (6) Moral Development (7) Spiritual Development.

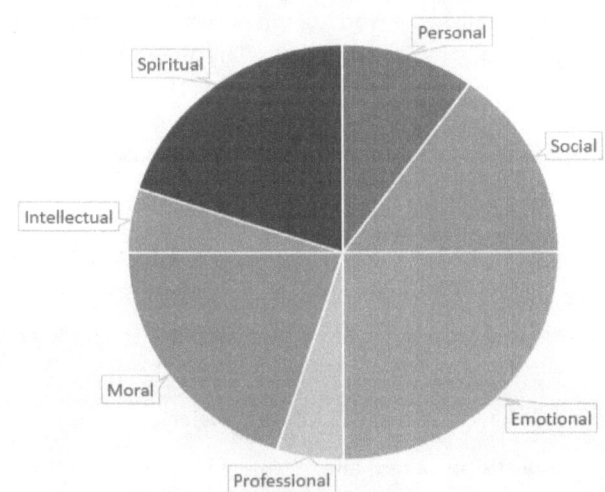

In reference to the above example, moral development is the cleaning of the shrubs and preparing the ground for laying the foundation of the spiritual aspect. The height of the building depends on the foundation. The more depth there is, the higher the building will be raised to greater heights. The emotional aspect is the bonding of the bricks using quality cement. The spiritual aspect is essential below ground, and the emotional aspect is important above ground. It is a sense of strong familyhood. If the cementing is not done correctly, soon there will be cracks. So, the emotional aspect weighs most amongst all the aspects above ground. The social aspect is the procurement after the cementing of emotions. The personal aspect pertains to painting. The professional aspect is developing skills; adding water works & electric facilities. The intellectual aspect is the landscaping and the gardening.

The Twin Tower collapse on 9/11, the mega-corporate scandals at WorldCom and Enron, and failure of large banking industries have frightened people. With advancements in technology, infrastructure & education the social and personal problems like AIDs, suicide, divorce, depression, stress are increasing. The reason for this is that we are far more focused on intellectual and professional aspects. We have focused on personal development to some extent, emotional and social even less; moral and spiritual aspects are receiving less attention, sometimes not at all.

It's not that we are not aware of it at all. Our discomfort and complaints have been expressed in several forms. Today, organizations have put a tremendous demand for authentic leaders that led to the development of Authentic Leadership style. This style focuses on authentic leaders and their authentic life and leadership. Organizations demand trustworthy people. Transformational Leadership also requires the transformation of self and others around. The Complete Leadership model encompasses all these with the development of seven aspects of an individual.

Pramukh Swami Maharaj could successfully develop these aspects in thousands of people. Most importantly, he established a working infrastructure to achieve this. He took an interest in people personally by meeting, counseling and serving them.

If we consider each aspect individually,

1. The personal aspect points to basic human characteristics, non-addiction, behavior, and discipline.
2. Intellectual aspect is concerned with education.
3. Professional aspect is concerned with the profession & skills development.
4. Emotional aspect refers to emotional stability in critical life events & sense of familyhood.
5. The social aspect is about how to live in a family and society.
6. Moral aspect is regarding ethical values, and
7. The spiritual aspect is to serve others, conquer one's ill temperaments like ego, anger, hatred, envy, etc.

In the following chapters, we will see how Swamiji could develop these aspects in his devotees and people at large.

> *"Average leaders raise the bar on themselves; good leaders raise the bar for others; great leaders inspire others to raise their own bar."*
> ~ Orrin Woodward ~

24. Personal Development

"The most powerful leadership tool you have is your own personal example."
~ John Wooden ~

The personal development is painting a house with decent colors. It is all about basic human characteristic, addiction-free life, behavior, and discipline. Before we paint a wall, we first need to plaster it. A basic human characteristic is like plastering, and then, enhanced behavior and discipline are painting over it.

Development of Basic Human Characteristics

On 25th December 1986, a business magnate Bhagubhai came for Swamiji's darshan in Mumbai. He said, "I have set up a factory to manufacture aluminum utensils in the tribal town of Selvas." Swamiji revealed, "We, too, have set up a factory there." A surprised Bhagubhai asked, "What type of factory is it?" Swamiji replied with a smile, "The factory transforms a person into a human being" (Pramukh Prasangam).

There are many kinds of industries – food industry, textile industry, beverage industry, the diamond industry, etc. But it was Pramukh Swamiji who had an industry to turn a person into a human being. A raw person would enter it and after a process turns into a human being. Here we are going to discuss the Selvas as an example. You will read how Swamiji developed basic human characteristics of this tribal community.

Selvas is a tribal area of Dadra and Nagar Haveli in South Gujarat India. The past of this tribal community was very primitive and dark. For centuries, they lived a life bereft of values and civility. But Swamiji took it on hand and today, thousands have been salvaged from the rut of ignorance, and now play to the tune of joy and enlightenment. They now live life by commercializing what they exploited from the jungles and the animals they hunted previously.

The tribal people lived on rice. They also lived on fish, which they caught from nearby streams. Also, they had nothing to wear except a loincloth. This was worn throughout the year; in the harsh heat, and rainy conditions. They carried bows, arrows, and slings to hunt birds and small animals for food. They cooked them on piles of twigs, igniting them by rubbing two stones together. Many tribals also resorted to stealing and dacoity to support their families. To forget their poverty and miseries, they took to drinking liquor by brewing it from *tad* and *mahuda* flowers and fruits. The vice of superstition and blind faith further blighted their lives and made them fearful. Treatment from witch doctors left them in even more agony and debt, and at times, led to death. Even their customs of marriage, death rites and other rituals proved to be exorbitant due to superstitions.

The pace of development and progress of the tribals was extremely sluggish. But the bleak situation soon changed drastically with the efforts of H.H. Pramukh Swami Maharaj and his sadhus, who traveled extensively in the tribal belt of Dadra and Nagar Haveli from 1971 onwards.

Narayanprasad Swami describes, "At that time we did not have a car. When we wanted to go from Vapi to Selvas, we traveled by public bus. It was always jam-packed because there was only one bus a day. We had to fast when we traveled by bus. In addition to the many passengers overcrowding the bus, some carried dead fish, making the journey intolerably revolting. No other vehicle could navigate the interior, narrow pathways. So, we sometimes had to walk long distances, 15 to 20 kilometers. The pathways in the jungle often posed many dangers. We would come across snakes and confront dacoits on the way. At night our troubles increased manifold, but despite that, we enjoyed inspiring Satsang among the tribals. We experienced that the tribals needed to be cheered and supported. They would be happy to see us. We would also go to see them when they were ailing, or when someone in the family had passed away. We offered prayers and also helped in mitigating their difficulties. Around 1979-80 we organized a seminar for teachers with Swamiji's blessings in which many gave up addictions and superstitions."

A veteran tribal, Ramubhai Makanbhai, who was once a sprightly youth volunteer, reminisces, "At that time our people were so poor, they did not have anything to cover the upper part of their body. They wore only a loincloth. Swamiji organized a campaign to distribute clothes to them. At Swamiji's behest, I used to go to villages to note the types and sizes of clothes that our people required. Then I would personally go to deliver them to each household. When I went to distribute raincoats and other clothes, they were overjoyed. I had never seen them so happy before. For five years they put on their raincoats before sleeping at night. The tribals felt fortunate they were given clothes to wear. Such was their feelings of joy. Swamiji arranged for free medical camps, mobile medical service for us. He started a school for us and managed everything we ever needed" (Opening of Swaminarayan Mandir, Selvas, 2013).

It was not only the tribal of Selvas which required to improve. Even people living in modern cities sometimes need to improve themselves.

On 30th April 2004 in London, Chandrakantbhai Pujara, a devotee, came with some of his relatives for Swamiji's darshan and blessings. Pointing to Amitkumar he said, "Bapa, he is studying Political Science."

"I want to do good for the world," said Amit.

Swamiji responded with appreciation, "Very good. To do good for our world is fine, but for that, you should pray to God daily. Then God will join you in fulfilling your wish. And secondly, you should live a pure, moral life. Despite pursuing political studies, you should remain steadfast in obeying God's laws. Be a vegetarian. Wherever you go never indulge in any form of addiction. If you follow this, then God will be with you, and you will always succeed" (Vicharan Report April 2004).

Addiction Free

Here are some surprising facts and figures related to addictions. Every year 50 lac (5 million) people die of smoking, out of which 4 lacs (400,000) die in the USA and 20 lacs (2 million) in India. Every day, 2000 die due to smoking in India alone; 82 deaths every hour. Every fifth death in the world is due to smoking. A German Sociologist has declared that 63% of physical struggles, 69% of asset related crime, 70% of sexual harassments, 70% of violent attacks are due to drunken people. In England alone every year, liquor is responsible for 5 lac (500,000) accidents (Pramukh Gnan Sarita, 2013).

Pramukh Swami Maharaj de-addicted people from alcohol, smoking, consumption of gutkha, etc. on a vast scale. He personally counseled people. On 24th June 2001, Swamiji was in Panchmadhi, India. The chief of the police training school, Mr. Mahesh Mudgal came to Swamiji. He had taken several measures to prevent addiction within the school. It did not seem to work. Finally, he had decided to give out strict penalties by suspending the officers on an experimental basis. However, the suspension made the lives of the officer's family miserable. He said to Swamiji, "None of our remedies works in stopping the addiction to alcohol, drugs & others. I hope that through holy men like you, you will be able to get rid of all the addiction."

Swamiji accepted his request and took him to a special meeting held for the police group. He gave them the teachings and blessings of religion, policy, honesty and virtuous life in Hindi. When Swamiji finished his speech, many of them took oaths:

'I will never lie.'

'I give up all the addictions today and won't take it in future.'

'I will serve poor to my might.'

'I will fulfill my responsibilities sincerely.'

'I won't get angry on others.'

Thus, where the many attempts of a high police officer failed, a pure speech from Swamiji worked. All the officers including Mr. Mudgal were overwhelmed. Instead of strict punishment, Swamiji could transform people through love and his real character (Sadhu P. , 2001).

Behavior and Discipline

Swamiji developed people for their behavior and discipline. It covered personal & public cleanliness; how to sit or stand; discipline at home, workplace, and public places.

Swamiji's motive was to lead everyone towards perfection washing out mistakes either by tongue, mind or action.

9th February, Atladra. A volunteer highlighted another volunteer's angry nature in a public assembly. Swamiji corrected him for doing so (Vicharan Report February 2005). 13th August 2008, In Chicago, a volunteer reported to Swamiji about some youths abusing one another. Swamiji called them and spent time with them to stop abusing. The youths apologized and promised they would not (Vicharan Report August 2008). Swamiji liked discipline whether it was about standing in a queue, about obeying traffic laws, government laws or respecting elders. He often corrected his followers to follow the rules and be disciplined.

Through his valuable tips, Swamiji could elevate people a step higher than their current stand. On 8th January 2007 in Ahmedabad, Raj Bhakta, a US congressman questioned Swamiji, "How can you inspire so many people to improve themselves? What we can do to inspire people around us?" Swamiji replied, "We should first practice what we say. Second, we should have a feeling to do good to all. Keep a perspective that everyone is noble, respect others then people will follow your advice" (Vicharan Report January 2007).

The above advice is invaluable to all those who want to lead. First, we need to develop our own personal aspect, and then we can change others'.

Complete Leadership

"Change yourself and others will follow."

~ Stephen Covery ~

25. Intellectual Development

"Intellectual development occurs best in a setting where people can share ideas freely, without censorship or fear of being ostracized."
~ Peter Gray ~

Intellectual development of a person is concerned with the education and providing an environment for it. In the previous chapter, we read how Swamiji developed the personal aspects of the tribal community at Selvas. Here we will see how he developed their educational aspect.

A few decades back one could not imagine tribal children enrolling in primary education. Pramukh Swami Maharaj inspired children to attend school. As a result, Lalubhai's son Ashok graduated as a doctor from M.S. University (Vadodara). Presently, he practices as a physician. Dr. Dipak and Dr. Sunil Daru, through the inspiration and support of Swamiji, have graduated as doctors. Many more male and female tribal youths are presently studying or have completed their studies in medicine or engineering. Dr. Prakash R. Patel, an agricultural scientist of national repute, is the first tribal of Dadra and Nagar Haveli to have acquired a Ph.D. in agriculture. He has written many research papers on agriculture (Opening of Swaminarayan Mandir, Selvas, 2013).

After Pramukh Swami Maharaj inaugurated the school in Selvas, thousands of tribal and other students have been receiving primary and secondary education. The students have excelled in carving out successful careers. The school has also been honored with national awards.

Intellectual development demands a high degree of concentration during studies. But, the intensity of media exposure is adversely affecting children's or youth's concentration. After 10 years of research on 1 lac (100,000) children, "National Institute of Mental Health" found that up to the age of 16, children see 1.5 lac

(150,000) violent scenes and 25,000 death scenes on TV. An American survey says, "83% children lose their childhood watching TV". A child spends 15,000 hours watching TV and 11,000 hours in school. In 1997, there was a survey question in the USA, "Whom do you like more? TV or your Mom?" 59% of the children liked TV! A 2012 paper published in Psychology of Popular Media Culture, has found that games while helping with a child's attention span by allowing to improve the concentration levels in short bursts, it did long-term damage to concentration (Pramukh Gnan Sarita, 2013).

The guardians (parents) are unable to guard their children against media attack. Swamiji could guard and guide this issue very well. On 13th May 2006 in Gondal, a boy asked Swamiji, "How can I concentrate on my studies?" Swamiji replied, "First, don't watch TV. Don't read anything that is unrelated to your studies. Do prayers. Give up wandering or seeing unnecessary and pointless things. Study properly. If you spend your entire vacation visiting others, then you will forget what you have learned. So, pay attention while reading, have restraint, and control your eating habits. Do not listen, read or see bad things. All these will enable you to concentrate" (Vicharan Report May 2006).

The above tips highlight Swamiji's philosophy of educational development. He actively restricted the use of smartphones at schools. There is a ban on TV, films, and games at the BAPS hostel. Respect for teachers, healthy eating practices aided in their educational development.

"The roots of education are bitter, but the fruit is sweet."
~ Aristotle ~

26. Professional Development

"It doesn't matter if you are a diamond or a lump of coal if you remain buried underground."
~ Anthony Marolt ~

In this materialistic era, people have emphasized this aspect so much that it has disrupted other aspects and caused tremendous stress or fierce competition. Blanchard in 'The Secret of Servant Leadership' weighed it only 20% and 80% to the character. In Complete Leadership model, Professional Development weighs decidedly very less compared to other aspects. Still, it is necessary for a person to make their livelihood. One must learn professional skills, and that too at world class perfection. But at the same time, we should keep in mind that we don't value or judge a person only for its professional aspect. Those who have developed their emotional, social, moral and spiritual aspects of life, value more over professional aspect. Though Swamiji believed in developing all the aspects, he valued moral and spiritual aspects most over others.

If we consider Swamiji through a professional aspect, Swamiji ran an NGO spread across the globe. He mastered each skill necessary for an organization to run successfully by doing the things himself for years and serving others. He mastered cooking to prepare food for the devotees, in arranging their accommodation, he would go to each room to check every faucet in the bathroom, lights, fans, bedsheets, blankets, cleanliness, ventilation, provision for mosquito and every tiny detail for the devotee's comfort. He would serve each devotee with due respect. He cared for their travel bookings, parking facilities, luggage security, their drivers, and much more. He also mastered other administrative departments such as accounts and legal aspects as well. He learned everything by doing it himself with an intention to serve the best. He knew what people would expect and how he could serve them best. He was an all-rounder servant who knew how to wash utensils correctly just as he knew how to polish the gold pinnacles of mandirs. As he learned by doing, he kept improving on it for years. Thus, he became the best trainer to develop thousands of volunteers and hundreds of sadhus for each of those services. Anything he did cross par excellence and became a milestone and ideal for others to follow and most importantly, do.

Servant leadership says, "Servant leaders are committed to helping each person in the organization grow personally and professionally. Commitment can take many forms, including providing followers with opportunities for career development, helping them develop new work skills, taking a personal interest in their ideas, and involving them in decision making" (Spears, 2002). Here we can see how Swamiji help develops the follower's skills.

Anandjivan Swamiji recalls his memories with Swamiji, "In 1981 Swamiji assigned me the responsibility to run children moral uplift activities. I knew its challenges as per my experiences during children's assemblies at Mumbai. I declined it. Swamiji said to me, "You must do it." In frustration, tears rolled from my eyes. Still, Swamiji assigned it to me. I was still with Swamiji for the next 15 days. I thought when I leave for Mumbai, again I will decline his offer. Then it was time to leave for Mumbai. Swamiji again said to me, "Now you are returning to Mumbai. There you should run the children activities with due responsibility. Take care of the children. Strengthen their moral and ethical values." His words, so gentle and still full of inspiration & support. I realize I might not be what I am today. I might have remained irresponsible forever" (Jeva Me Nirkhya Re - 7, 1995, p. 44).

For any professional activity, spirituality should be its foundation. Swamiji started a school with 2000 students in Sarangpur. Punyakirti Swami was looking after its administrative activities. On 13th April 2001, he requested Swamiji to give a message to the students. Swamiji said, "Work peacefully with all. Gradually participate in moral assemblies. Do not hurry." Then he instructed Punyakirti Swami, "Don't penalize the students. The penalty doesn't improve the students. The student will pay the penalty because his father earns. But then he would not be comfortable with us. Work with love and affection" (Vicharan Report April 2001).

A young man requested, "Bless me to be creative." Swamiji was pleased and said, "You requested the best of the best. You will succeed in business, as creativity is what you will deliver. The business will grow accordingly, and people will be happy too. Swamiji gave him the advice to grow professionally. He also added, 'If you pray daily, then it will help you be creative."

Many organizations work in tribal areas to convert them to their religion through financial or educational aids. Swamiji also worked in those areas, but he has not converted a single person for any gain. Among the many tribal areas, there is one area called Ukai, in Gujarat. Swamiji runs a hostel there for poor tribal children. There are no prospects of any return to BAPS from this area. Swamiji had been working there for the last 40 years, to serve them for their intrinsic value. Once Swamiji visited the area. He inquired about every minute detail. Swamiji knew that every kid doesn't like powder milk. He instructed to arrange for cow or buffalo milk. He also suggested to cover the rough blanket surface with soft covers to protect the kid's skin, and also told the administrator to modify the playground surface to flatten it for the comfort of the kid's (Vicharan Report 2003).

Swamiji cared for kids as a mother and the necessities as a father.

Bhadra is a small village with a population of a mere 2000. Swamiji built a marvelous mandir there. On 11th January 2001, one of the devotees Jagdishbhai Busa reported, "Here we don't have anyone who can give a speech to the audience." Swamiji said, "Tell volunteers to memorize five Swami ni vato. Initially, narrate those before everyone. Let them speak for 10-15 minutes initially. Eventually, they will be prepared for assembly speech" (Vicharan Report January 2001, p. 89).

Servant leadership fosters the development of a community. A community is a collection of individuals who have shared interests and pursuits and felt a sense of unity and relatedness. A community allows followers to identify with something greater than themselves that they value. Servant leaders build a community to provide a place where people can feel safe and connected with others but are still allowed to express their individuality.

> "Life is growth. If we stop growing, technically and spiritually, we are as good as dead."
>
> ~ Morihei Ueshiba ~

27. Emotional Development

"If you are tuned out of your own emotions, you will be poor at reading them in other people."
~ Daniel Goleman ~

Emotional development is about controlling one's emotions. Scientists talk about the open loop system. An open-loop system is mostly dependent on external sources. The blood circulation system of our body is a closed loop system. It can work independently irrespective of the outer world. But our emotions rely on our relationship with other people. We call it an open loop system. Our emotions affect others, and other's affect us. Research in intensive care units has shown that the presence of a loving person lowers the victim's blood pressure and slows down the secretion of fatty acids that block arteries. Three or more severe stress incidents may triple the death rate in a socially isolated person (Goleman, 2004).

Emotions play an essential role in our life. A person who can't control anger, envy or other such emotions ruins the atmosphere around and the work culture as well. Many people have come to Pramukh Swamiji and regretted theirs out of control emotions.

A military commander met Swamiji and said, "I can control the enemies, but I am unable to control my anger. Please bless me."

Once Swamiji was traveling by Singapore Airlines from Auckland to Singapore. During the flight, Kirtan a boy of thirteen asked Swamiji a few questions.

Kirtan: I get outraged! How can I overcome it?

Swamiji: Wherever you get angry, start praying. Chant 'Swaminarayan... Swaminarayan.' If you pray before God, your anger will subside. Now, think, where is the need to get angry? There is no gain being angry with anyone. By getting angry, your work is not done. The other person is left miserable and distressed. By singing hymns, chanting Swaminarayan, Swaminarayan the distress of the other person and yours, is dissolved.

Kirtan: I am very lazy. How can I get rid of lethargy?

Swamiji: That you shouldn't have at all. How can you be lazy at such a young age? If you have laziness at this age, then you won't be able to study and will never get a good job. Laziness is your enemy. Think like this and get rid of it. Wake up early in the morning. Engage yourself in prayer and study. You should not be lazy in any work. Don't say 'later.' Do your work 'now.' Don't leave your studies, lessons, your prayers for tomorrow or later. Do it today.

After a while, Swamiji asked Kirtan, "Now I'll ask you a question. When you grow up, will you be as good as you are now? Because children get spoilt when they grow up. They don't come to prayer meetings; don't perform puja and they get into bad company. God will be happy and grant you spiritual liberation if you attend religious assemblies in your life. Kirtan promised Bapa that he would attend spiritual meetings all his life" (Shelat, 2017).

The temperament of a teacher was very high. Once he was away in the afternoon, and his daughter started the radio. The teacher didn't like it and lost his temper. He smashed the radio to pieces. The shopkeeper said that no one can repair it now. On another occasion, the teacher's son's examination was nearing. So, he asked his son to prepare for the exam, but the boy took it lightly and decided to go out on his bicycle. On seeing this, the teacher got angry with his son. In his anger, he smashed the bicycle and made it unusable. The boy took the bicycle to the sell it as scrap. The shopkeeper had never seen anything like this in his life.

But all this changed when the teacher met Swamiji in Bochasan. He confessed his anger to Swamiji. Swamiji blessed him. After a few months following Swamiji's advice, he got rid of his rage and anger. He told Swamiji, "My anger has now almost vanished. You have transformed my life" (Brahmopanishad, 1992, p. 101).

Swamiji helped thousands of people conquer their emotions and live a peaceful and happy life.

> *"Leadership means forming a connection with people at an emotional level."*
> *~ Adeo Consulting ~*

28. Social Development

*"Be a good human being, a warmhearted, affectionate person.
This is my fundamental belief."*
~ Dalai Lama ~

Along with materialistic development, there is a collapse. Why are suicide rates much high there? Why are old age homes are increasing? Why are divorce cases growing exponentially? Why are people with Aids rising at an alarming rate? Why are child-parent problems crossing the boundary?

What we need is a civilized and, cultured developed country! Only then can our lives be peaceful and self-content. Materialistic development doesn't lead to happiness. As a child's body grows in proportion to age, everything in the nation should grow in proportion. With prosperity, the character should grow, mutual sympathy should grow, and spirituality should grow as well.

If there are good roads in the country, cars will travel smoothly. But if the driver is drunk, the accident rate will be high.

So, it poses several questions:

Why do they drink? Some people drink because they are not happy.
Why not happy? Because of some family or work problems!
Why family or work problems? Lack of cultural values and moral values!
Why lack of moral values? It's not taught at home or school!

However, it is taught by spiritual leaders. Pramukh Swami Maharaj was such a spiritual leader who worked for transforming and edifying the lives of people continuously.

A change was ushered in the life of Rishubha of Talaja through a home visit by Swamiji. The unscrupulous Darbars of Sangana village took a happier, peaceful turn in life after two hours of spiritual association with Swamiji. And Maganbhai Samani's 54 years of stubborn addiction to smoking vanished in the two days that Swamiji stayed at his house. Lakha Lulla and his two sons turned vegetarian under Swamiji's advice. Even the tribal of Panchmahal and Selvas districts and the pariahs of Sandeshar and several other villages were cleansed of their immoral ways by Swamiji's purity. In the district of Dadra and Nagar Haveli, many villages have been transformed. They chopped off trees from which they brewed beer and planted new saplings. This had to be done so that their children and future generations will not even have an inkling of their former unethical lives. The tribal people have given up promiscuity, superstition and false godmen. The practice of sacrificing hens at the fulfillment of a wish has stopped. Even the vile practice of killing a hen or goat for the success of a marriage ceremony has been given up. Without any distinctions of class, creed or country, Swamiji has through his efforts ushered in a peaceful edification and sanctified the huts and homes of hundreds and thousands. He believed that mere speeches or discourses impress and inform but to transform people, one has to meet them with love on an individual, person to person basis. And that is why through his perennial travels he has touched the hearts of countless people.

Sunsar is a cheeky village in the Patan district, Gujarat. People at Sunsar were famous for the robbery and alcoholic addictions. When a crime was committed, the police would suspect that the culprit was from this village, but wouldn't dare go there and catch any of them. One of Swamiji's devotees Dr. Desai went to Sunsar and started counseling people for a better life. Eventually, the entire village transformed. People began living an addiction-free and moral life. Like Sunsar, Swamiji altered hundreds of villages to lead people to live happily, with prosperity and live in the moral confines.

After an operation in Mumbai to remove a benign tumor, Swamiji recuperated at Parmanandbhai Patel's bungalow for 15 days. His stay ushered in a change in the lives of the entire family and their servants. In the town of Kosamba, Valsad district, thousands of fishermen and their families have become devotees and have thus abstained from robbery & mischief to others.

Just as doctors, ministers, businessmen, laborers, and others contribute to our society, likewise, the sadhus play a priceless role in elevating and purifying society. Miscreants are tried and put behind bars, but this does not dissolve their criminal propensities. The task of enabling their lives rests upon holy sadhus. This mission of Swamiji was carried out through his tireless travels – washing away the dirt of corruption and vices (Viveksagardas, 1997).

> *"It is not enough to be compassionate. You must act."*
>
> *~ Dalai Lama ~*

29. Moral / Ethical Development

"Morality is the basis of things and the truth is the substance of all morality."
~ Mahatma Gandhi ~

Greenleaf mentioned 'Awareness' as one of the characteristics of a servant leader. General awareness, and especially self-awareness, strengthen the servant leader. Awareness helps one in understanding issues involving ethics, power, and values. It lends itself to being able to view most situations from a more integrated, holistic position (Blanchard & Broadwell, Servant Leadership in Action).

Someone asked Swamiji for his message for society. Swamiji said, "Become ethical and formulate an ethical society" (Kjdas, 1997). The summary of Pramukh Swamiji's life & work can be as, "He lived a pure ethical life, transformed thousands of people to live an ethical life and provided a sound structure for that." Pramukh Swamiji could understand ethical issues and foresee the consequences of it. He firmly believed that a lack of ethics is the root cause of most problems. He established a network to conduct more than 20,000 assemblies a week around the world to inspire people to live ethically. He could engage one million children, youths and elders in his movement. He provided a novel concept of 'Gharsabha' where the family eats together, pray together and learn ethical values for peace and harmony. People at large learned and strengthened ethical values at those centers. He built more than 1000 mandirs and initiated around 12,000 cultural centers for it.

Being ethical is to keep our vows: Bhagwanji Mandavia was a dynamic business administrator in Toronto. Active in the Indo-Canada Federation, and guiding the Gujarati community, Bhagwanji was enjoying success at its best (Pramukh Swami Maharaj - The Inspirer and Instiller of Philosophy in Life, 2004). He was invited to a banquet, arranged to honor Queen Elizabeth in Toronto. Bhagwanjibhai practiced a strict vow of vegetarianism. He declined the invitation to the prestigious event. No one would dream to cancel such an invitation! The invitees, pleased with his vow, provided vegetarian food for him.

Atlantic City is a gambling city. One who goes there will play. There are some followers of Swamiji's who work at the casinos but have never played. Staying in that environment and resisting one's mind is challenging. These followers kept their vow to Swamiji that they won't gamble, ever (Sadhu V. , 1992, p. 111).

Global statistics of HIV reports that more than 70 million people have been infected with the HIV virus and about 35 million people have died of HIV. Globally, 36.9 million [31.1–43.9 million] people were living with HIV at the end of 2017. An estimated 0.8% [0.6-0.9%] of adults aged 15–49 years worldwide are living with HIV, although the burden of the epidemic continues to vary considerably between countries and regions. The WHO African region remains most severely affected, with nearly 1 in every 25 adults (4.1%) living with HIV.

The steps are taken mostly for the cure and secure. There are no measures to deal it through self-restraint. If a person is moral and self-refrain, then there will be less to deal with precautionary measures.

Today, sexual assault is a significant issue at secondary schools, colleges, and workplaces. There are around 250,000 recorded cases per year (Sexual Assault, n.d.). Teaching moral lessons from childhood regarding this is essential. At BAPS cultural centers children and youth are taught to control their senses and practice celibacy until marriage. The children and youth keep a distant from friendships and pre-marriage relationships.

There are hundreds of such examples, let me describe a one here.

Alpesh Mangukiya studied at a BAPS hostel in Surat. Many girls wanted to be friends with him. But, with the moral lessons learned from Pramukh Swamiji, he did not become friends with the girls. He entirely focused on his studies (Vicharan Report April 2005). Today, thousands of youth (men and women) at BAPS practice celibacy till marriage and show deep respect for this ideal.

Some countries have over 20% of its population who are HIV positive. Worldwide more than 1 million people die of AIDs every year. The steps are taken mostly for a cure and secure. There are no measures to deal it through self-restraint. If a person is moral and self-refrain, then there will be less to deal with precautionary measures.

Persuasion is another trait of a servant leader as described by Greenleaf. He says, "Persuasion is clear and persistent communication that convinces others to change. As opposed to coercion, which utilizes positional authority to force compliance, persuasion creates change through the use of gentle, nonjudgmental argument" (Northouse, Leadership: Theory and Practice, 2016).

Pramukh Swamiji through his persuasion could radically change the lives of people at large. Here is an example:

Sokhda is a small village near Matar in Kheda district, Gujarat, India. A devotee Purusottamdas invited Swamiji to stay at his village. There was only one convenient house in the village for Swamiji's stay; the home of the village chief Jashbhai's. Jashbhai had a strong repulsion for sadhus. He bluntly disliked them. After several requests, he agreed, but on the condition that he will go elsewhere for the duration of Swamiji's stay there. Pramukh Swamiji stayed at Jashbhai's house for two days. On departing, Swamiji asked, "Whose house is this? Call the owner."

Purusottamdas explained, "It belongs to the village chief Jashbhai, but he has gone elsewhere due to hatred for sadhus." If we stay in his house, don't we have to thank him?" Swamiji replied. Finally, Purusottamdas brought Jashbhai. He was fuming with rage. But on seeing Swamiji, he fell at his feet. "O God!" he cried. "Won't you stay another two days in my house? Please?"

Swamiji stayed there for two more days. Only Jashbhai knew what he had experienced, but he came out the better for it. It transformed his life. He gave all addictions and led a virtuous life thereafter (Anandswaroopdas, 1998, p. 66). It's said that 'Silence is a universal language.' Swamiji was used to talk less. He mastered the silent communication to change others. On 18th January 1995, Swamiji was in Ahmedabad. Physiotherapist Dr. Dilipbhai Patel had come to meet Swamiji. He said, "I find that you convey goodness by your mere presence. Your silence can dismiss doubts. You speak little, but it is very persuasive. It reaches into the heart." (Anandswaroopdas, 1998).

In June 2001, Abdul Kalam said Swamiji, "Swamiji, it's a pity that good citizens are not produced by the laws of the Government. They are created only by Swamiji's like you." Yes, only a moral person who lives moral life can inspire others for same.

> *"No matter how educated, talented, rich, or cool you believe you are, how you treat people ultimately tells all. Integrity is everything."*
> *~ Unknown ~*

30. Spiritual Development

"Our scientific power has outrun our spiritual power. We have guided missiles and misguided men."
~ Martin Luther King, Jr. ~

Spiritual development rests at the peak of all other developments. It's the highest for any human being. It surpasses all other achievements. It's a purity of mind and soul. Its only through spiritual practice one can conquer ego, hatred and other passions. The spiritual aspect is concerned with developing virtues like non-violence, tolerance, mercy and serving others selflessly. Pramukh Swami Maharaj was spiritually pure so that he could develop spiritual aspect of people. We have a picture in our mind for only elders should think of spiritual development. But Swamiji believed spiritual teachings necessary for all and especially from childhood. He inspired thousands of kids and youth for spiritual development through spiritual discourses, assemblies, and activities serving others selflessly.

Serve Selflessly

Swamiji's guidance developed many people from zero to hero. Those who were a headache for the family and society were transformed and started serving others.

Ramanbhai and Gulabbhai's stories are unique in the small Wahial village of Kaprada area near Valsad. They used to drink alcohol all day long. No one dared to stop them. Once they wanted to drink, but their pockets were empty. Both of them became restless. They saw a man driving his cart. They caught him and demanded money. He refused and was beaten up. His money was snatched and used for alcohol consumption.

During the monsoon, they went to the forests of Nashik in Maharashtra and smuggled large wood trunks. They would sit on them and swim back on it through the river to their village early in the morning. Sometimes the bullets of forest officials went through them, but they disregarded it. The people around and state police were afraid of them.

Swamiji took the case on hand. After a few moral assemblies, they gave up all their ills and started living a pious life. Today, there are several volunteers from this village. They are serving people for their moral and spiritual upliftment.

There are hundreds of villages wholly transformed. They now live moral and spiritual lives. Some have become model villages to inspire others. In 11th March 2005, Mahelav's Vicharan Report on Swamiji records Petli village as an example. After Swamiji started moral activities here, it is now a village free of any addictions, and for the last twenty years, it is also crime-free. There is not a single recorded case with the local police. The government had awarded it a 'Tirthgram' award. Dahyabhai wins every term in the elections without anyone against him for his selfless services and moral life as an example to others.

Children most often spend their vacation playing games and watching TV or films and sometimes on an outing. Swamiji encouraged them to join the de-addiction campaign during their vacation. At BAPS cultural centers they are trained and then set out to make people aware of addictions. In 2007, around 35,000 children participated in de-addiction campaigns, contacted 3 million people and de-addicted one million of them from tobacco, alcohol, and smoking.

Non-violence is a common characteristic found in great world leaders. Swamiji also possessed it. A Muslim butcher Ayyub came to Swamiji and apologized for his slaughter business. Swamiji blessed him to give up this business and stay on the path of non-violence. Swamiji always said, "If we cannot give life to anyone, we don't have the right to take away."

Conquer Ego

At Akshardham, Gandhinagar, there was a multimedia show produced by Prof. Fritch from Czechoslovakia. Someone asked him, "Why is your name not mentioned in the show?" He replied, "I am not a fool. Swamiji has not written his name anywhere in Akshardham. How can I write mine?" The great scientist and late president of India accepted Swamiji as his spiritual teacher and exclusively wrote a book 'Transcendence' on him. There he mentioned, "Swamiji is my ultimate teacher who taught me how to remove 'I' and 'Me' (Kalam & Tiwari, 2015).

Tolerate

Swamiji could transform his followers to develop tolerance and put it in practice. Narayanbhai Faldu is a social worker and volunteer in Jamnagar rural area. He travels to nearby villages for the social & spiritual upliftment of people. Once he went to a village Bhanvad and visited a house there. The elderly person present had some prejudice for social reformers. He abused him and hit Narayanbhai. Without any reaction, Narayanbhai left silently. After a few days, Narayanbhai again went to the same house and met that person who abused him. Narayanbhai's tolerance transformed the person, and he apologized for his behavior.

Pramukh Swami Maharaj was a great spiritual scientist who guided followers to outpace their evil passions and enlighten their inner beauty.

Unity

"Unity is strength... when there is teamwork and collaboration, wonderful things can be achieved."

~Mattie Stepanek~

Unity is a great spiritual virtue. It is necessary for any team to succeed. Pramukh Swami Maharaj could bring unity to such a level that his followers could work together and stay together. Today, there is a crisis in the world; of broken families. Swamiji set an example at the Sarangpur Training Center where 300 Sadhus live together as a family, dine in a single kitchen without any discrimination of nationality, caste, race, color or religion. They study together, work together, stay together with great affection and respect for each other. The Saint Training Center at Sarangpur resides at the peak of Swamiji's creation and development – a model for everyone to learn and live.

Obey Scriptures

Obeying moral laws from scriptures is a human duty. As we obey traffic laws; stand in a queue at public places; follow discipline at workplaces, schools, colleges; obey many other government laws to run the systems smoothly. These laws and controls are essential, discouraging them may put us in chaos. The same is true for laws described in our scriptures. Pramukh Swami Maharaj inspired thousands of people to obey the laws described in the scriptures of the community they belonged to.

"Just as a candle cannot burn without fire, men cannot live without a spiritual life."
~ Buddha ~

31. Implementation

"It's not about perfect. It's about effort; and when you implement that effort into your life ... Every single day, that's where transformation happens. That's how change occurs. Keep going. Remember why you started."
~ *Goal Getting Podcast* ~

We have talked about the seven development aspects. Usually, there is a theory and then its practical implementation. But surprisingly, Swamiji implemented the practical side first, and the theory was developed out of it. In regards to implementation, one can learn from the existing processes and infrastructure developed by Swamiji. Swamiji explored the way to implement it in June 2001 in Delhi. The late Indian president Dr. APJ Abdul Kalam, the father of India's first nuclear bomb, the architect of our sophisticated space and missile technology, and a rare scientist whose vision to develop society upon the foundation of values met Swamiji in Delhi that day.

Dr. Kalam: "India is a developing country. It means economically it is not strong, socially it is not stable, security is not enough... that is called a developing country. Five hundred members like me are thinking, what should be the next vision for India? How do we transform a developing country into a developed country in the next 30 years? We have identified five important areas to transform India: Education & Healthcare, Agriculture, Information & Communication, Infrastructure, and Critical Technology. Swamiji, our problem is that we can present this before the Government, but how do we create people with values to carry out such a big vision. What we need is a cadre of value-based citizens. For this, you are an expert. We need your advice."

Swamiji: Along with these five, add a sixth - faith in God and developing people through spirituality. This is very important. We need first to generate a moral and spiritual atmosphere. We need to raise people who live by the laws of the scriptures and bear faith in God."

Dr. Kalam: Swamiji, for carrying forward such a big vision of transforming India, should we first create a spiritual tradition, make people spiritual and then embark upon our vision, or focus on one of the critical areas like education or health? Or should we integrate everything and begin simultaneously?

Swamiji: Simultaneously. Work in the five fields you have identified for the country's progress should be continued, and together with it, this should be parallelly incorporated.

Dr. Kalam: To realize this great dream, three types of people are needed - Punya Atma (virtuous people), Punya Neta (virtuous leaders) and Punya Adhikari (virtuous officers). If the population of all the three increase in our society, then India would become the Jagadguru (world leader). How can their numbers be increased?

Swamiji: Together with your academic and scientific efforts, give spiritual training in our schools and colleges. Nowadays, spiritual education has been removed from schools and colleges. That which should be received from infancy is not being given, and we continue to teach mere academic knowledge only. But from the beginning, right from birth, people should be taught values, only then will people become virtuous. From the cradle, such values should be inspired. In the education syllabus, knowledge of our scriptures and great sadhus and sages should be given. Such a system will help produce virtuous people. The virtuous social, spiritual and political leaders we see today have attained their values from the very beginning. In the past, such values were taught in our gurukul system of education. Whether a prince or a pauper, everyone studied together. Along with academics, lessons such as Satyam Vada (speak the truth), Dharmam Chara (tread the path of righteousness), service towards others and faith in God, were taught.

Dr. Kalam: Swamiji, good citizens, are not produced by the laws of the Government. They are created only by Swamijis like you. Can you preach to families that up to the age of 15, parents should take an interest in their children and inspire values in them? Similarly, in all elementary schools, teachers should also teach values to their pupils. But if we miss this age of 15 of instilling values by father, mother, and teacher, then the Government cannot produce good honest citizens. Is my understanding correct?

Swamiji: Yes, it's true. It's definitely true. We've been saying this from the very beginning that values should be taught by parents at home, teachers at school and the guru in life (Fusion of Science and Spirituality, 2001).

We have some leadership theories like Authentic Leadership, Ethical Leadership and Transformational Leadership that focus on the development of people, but these don't explore an effective plan and required infrastructure to develop just and moral people. The implementation of Complete Development is not a matter of implementation at the workplace. It's a collective effort where leader, followers, parent, teachers, entrepreneurs and government's participation is required. It cannot be a training session of a few days or a month. It's a continuous ongoing process. One has to start with oneself. I am discussing more on the development of emotional, social, moral and spiritual aspects because the other already have enough awareness created, and people are practicing it. To implement the other four successfully following are needed.

(1) **Motive:** One's inner drive behind any action or activity should be based on 'In Joy of others, lies our own. In progress of others lies our own.'

(2) **An Ideal:** Complete development is a development of self. It requires an ideal present before us because people learn by example rather quickly over reading books or discourses. Other factors work, but a living example is most effective. We can see children are fast learners, they learn by people around them. They learn a language without attending any school. They learn it through direct exposure. Therefore, if one can find a living example, then learning and practicing will be quick. If it is not available, then one can learn it through reading books or listening to stories of great ideal leaders.

(3) **Cultivate a Sense of Familyhood:** Yogiji Maharaj called it 'Suhrudaybhav.' It's a feeling or attachment we possess for our family members that is unconditional love, selfless service, sacrifice, motivational support, responsibility, and empathy. With our family members, we feel a sense of myness, an attachment. To become a leader, one needs to extend it to a large group and keep extending it to the world as one family. To create a sense of familyhood one can start with the following:

   a. Meet your group members & subordinates
   b. Arrange a get-together
   c. Invite them to a social event
   d. Serve them
   e. Eat together, pray together at least once a day

      f.   Try to know their likes and dislikes, and act or serve accordingly

      g.   Try practicing and implementing familyhood traits described earlier

(4) **Daily Exposure to Moral & Spiritual Experiences**: A person's development completely depends on their exposure. They become what they see, read and listen. The implementation of Complete Leadership requires to stop non-moral and non-spiritual exposure and increase moral and spiritual exposure. One can increase it by watching, reading and listening to moral stories. The group should sit together and arrange a moral assembly for it at regular interval. At BAPS it is called 'Satsang.'

(5) **Charity Begins at Home**: Before helping others, one should practice this in their own home. One should start with respecting their parents (Bow to them with folded hands), understand their sacrifice and services, obey them, serve them. Then, respect people all around you.

(6) **Create an Environment**: Thinking good of others creates an ideal positive environment, and it affects others respect and join us. Highlight your subordinate's positive points or strengths and hide the negative ones. Put them ahead of you, consider their opinions, appreciate them for their accomplishments, forget & forgive their mistakes.

(7) **Track your Progress**: Track your progress whether it aligns with your motive as mentioned in point (1) in the joy of others.... Introspect your actions and decisions according to it. Also, measure it with the outcome of peace. Are your actions and decisions leading you toward peace of mind or not?

(8) **Infrastructure**: Try to provide the infrastructure as described in chapter 'Infrastructure' or join any existing ready infrastructure which can fulfill your emotional, social, moral and spiritual needs.

> *"All you need is the plan, the road map, and the courage to press on to your destination."*
> *~ Earl Nightingale ~*

32. Complete Leadership Questionnaire

The questionnaire here determines one's Complete Leadership Index. It has six sections with 70 questions in reference to the Complete Leadership Model. The model is applicable to a person, a family, small or big sized organization, institutions, a country, and the world.

- Each question weights 7 points. If you don't agree at all then select zero, if you agree very little with it you can weigh it either 1 or 2 points.
- If you agree 50% to it, then weigh it either 3 or 4 points.
- If you agree 60-80% to it, then weigh it 5 points.
- If you strongly agree with it, then you can weigh it 6 or 7 points.
- Repeat it for all the questions through section A to section F. At the end, sum your points for each section and place it in the formula given at the end of the questionnaire.
- Calculate the formula, and it will show your Complete Leadership grade.

Core Questionnaire (A)

1. I respect people as human beings over nationality, religion, caste, gender, department or any other discrimination
2. The sacrifice I make for my family members or dear ones, I can do the same for large groups (organization, community, and nation) to the same degree
3. Friends or enemies – I can treat all with the same respect and do good for all
4. I feel happy when my competitors progress

5. I can work among rivals with peace of mind and stability
6. I understand the value of inner peace and salvation over the materialistic success

Basic Leadership Traits Questionnaire (B)

7. A person must practice honesty at any cost
8. One should avoid pre-marital sex
9. One should be loyal to his/her marriage partner and avoid sex with others
10. Never take a bribe even if there are no chances of being caught
11. One should not make money using others
12. One should share organization profits with employees or subordinates
13. A leader should not exploit powers to get the work done
14. I can forgive if someone insults me
15. Friends or enemies – I can treat all with the same respect and do good to all
16. I believe character to be more important than money and power
17. Luxuries, a high- lifestyle is not the measure of success
18. One should respect both the rich and poor to the same degree
19. I apologize for my mistakes to my younger fellows/subordinates
20. Politeness always works more effectively over the use of power
21. One who harms me, I still think good of him/her and help them
22. Though someone criticizes me, I can still give them a key position as per their talent
23. I have no prejudice or discrimination of caste, religion, country, gender or race
24. I don't compromise moral values even if there is social pressure
25. I always support the truth at the cost of my position, wealth and reputation
26. Attractions or other benefits never deviate me from my goal
27. I can be patient and stand stable in any tragedy
28. I can encourage/motivate the team for difficult goals/ task very effectively
29. People trust me to resolve their conflicts, and they settle their conflicts easily

Familyhood Traits Questionnaire (C)

30. At workplace or home - my inner drive is to serve others selflessly. I have no craving for fame, money, awards, appreciation or any other reason except to serve others
31. I care for my subordinates when they are ill
32. I visit and sit with my subordinates if they are facing any work difficulties
33. I listen more than I talk. I listen to the problems of others very attentively and try to solve those sincerely
34. I can feel the difficulties of others as I feel my own
35. I provide emotional support to my team/group in case they lose, underperform or become depressed
36. I respect other's opinions and suggestions
37. I feel every one as my family member in my team/group
38. I always sacrificed my comforts to facilitate others or to fulfill their demands
39. As a leader, I take responsibility for failures and don't blame others for it

Field Specific Traits Questionnaire (D)

Case: You are alone on a trip, barefoot in a jungle. On the way, you meet a stranger. He is very weak due to dysentery and can't walk further. He has $10,000 cash with him. Your pockets are empty. He is crying for help. Both of you don't have any mobile phone. No one else can help him there in the dense jungle. It requires your two months of volunteering service to save the stranger. He is not going to give you a single penny from his $10,000 cash.

40. You have your ambitions and targets ahead. Will you help him and stay there for two months in such conditions?

There is no shelter available. An old banyan tree in a scary place is used as a shelter. There are ghostly voices at night.

41. Will you dare stay there to serve this stranger?

Due to the stranger's delicate health, you have to construct a two feet soft bed out of banana leaves. You have to go and collect at least 500 leaves and prepare a bed for him.

42. Will you do it enthusiastically?

He is suffering from frequent dysentery. You have to wash and bathe the stranger without gloves. You will have to replace the banana leaves and prepare his bed frequently to maintain hygiene.

43. Will you enjoy serving him like this?

There is no vehicle available. Nearby there is no city so that you can admit him at any hospital. If you want to feed him, you need to walk to a distant village every day to bring some food back for him.

44. Will you enthusiastically walk for him 10 miles a day?

The stranger has specific food wishes. There is no refrigerator to prepare the food once which can then be stored for a few days. There is no gas fuel or any other equipment available. You need to collect dry woods and set fire to cook the food. The smoke may tear your eyes.

45. Will you cook fresh food for him every day?

He is very selfish. He gives you a fixed amount that can only buy the ingredients for him. He finishes everything, and nothing is left for you. He doesn't care to ask you what you will eat? You have to again walk to the nearby village and beg food for yourself. Sometimes when people don't donate anything, you will have fast that day.

46. Will you tolerate it and continue to serve him?

After two months he is recovered and can carry his luggage for the journey ahead. Though he is stronger than you, still he asks you to carry his luggage. You have to carry 40 pounds on your back and follow him barefooted for the next 650 km.

47. Will you show the courtesy to carry his luggage even though he is capable of it?

You served him with all the above conditions. He doesn't thank you or appreciates you through words or any financial rewards.

48. Is it possible that you don't feel any misery or pity about it and remain happy as before?

The stranger has taken your services, didn't pay you anything, didn't care for your food, and sometimes you didn't find any food and fasted for many days. Still,

49. You won't have a single ill-thought for him.
50. Will you pray to God to bless him?

51. You won't tell anyone about your great humanitarian service and the stranger's awkward behavior to anyone for years to come.
52. You didn't expect anything in return the moment you started serving him. No wages, no payment, no appreciation, no thanks, nothing.
53. You think that I served and helped him selflessly, with this God will be pleased and bless me in return

    (The story above may appear impractical and exaggerated, but it's actually true! Nilkanth Varni (Lord Swaminarayan) served a sadhu named Sevakram for two months in 1797. The full story on page 59, http://download.baps.org/books/NilkanthCharitra-eng.pdf)

Qualities of a Selfless Servant (E)

54. You dislike praise or appreciation for your selfless service. You can serve others despite their negative comments.
55. You can balance your personal moral and spiritual life while serving others
56. Inner drive to serve is the motivating factor behind your services – it's not ego or any other material gain concerning money or anything else
57. You can serve compromising your schedules, timings, likes, and dislikes
58. You can serve your comforts to others, and you suffer miserable conditions (i.e., you have limited food and a group hunting for food arrives. You give it all to them and tolerate the hunger)
59. You pass the credits of your achievements and services to your subordinates or team members
60. You can serve for a lifetime with the same enthusiasm without any holiday or Sunday with the qualities and conditions mentioned above
61. You never feel tired of serving others. You enjoy it. You feel relaxed serving others. Playing, eating, swimming, mountaineering, outing, trips or any other amusements does not give you that excitement which serving others gives you.
62. You can prepare a team of such selfless servants with the qualities above

Overall Development Questionnaire (F)

63. How much necessity do you feel for the development of all seven aspects?
64. How good is your setup for personal development?
65. How good is your setup for intellectual development?

66. How good is your setup for professional development?
67. How good is your setup for emotional development?
68. How good is your setup for social development?
69. How good is your setup for moral development?
70. How good is your setup for spiritual development?

Put your totals for each section into following formula.

CLI = (A x 0.25) + (B x 0.20) + (C x 0.15) + (D x 0.10) + (E x 0.10) + (F x 0.20)

Check the value of CLI (Complete Leadership Index) with the table below. It reveals your score.

Grade	Score
A	441–393
B	392–344
C	343–295
D	294–246
E	245–197
F	196–148
G	147–100

33. The Complete Leadership Grid

The Complete Leadership Grid is a somewhat unique grid compared to other conventional grids. It has multiple X-axis and multiple Y-axis. We will see it through two figures. The first figure contains two X-axis and a Y-axis. The Y-Axis represents the core values of the model – Familyhood, Common Good and Peace. The X-Axis represents the seven aspects of development. These aspects are divided into two groups. (1) Phase 1: Moral Development and Spiritual Development. (2) Phase 2: Personal Development, Intelligence Development,

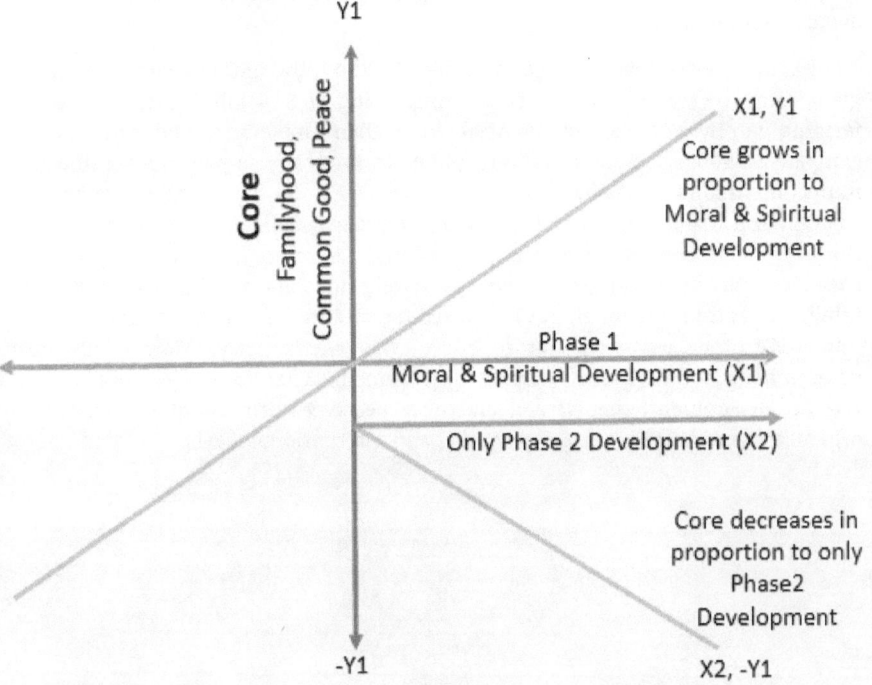

Professional Development, Social Development and Emotional Development. Phase 1 is represented on the X1 axis, and Phase 2 is measured on the X2 axis.

The grid also illustrates the negative axis of X1 and Y1. The negative axis measures the negative value for each.

The above grid shows the importance of moral and spiritual development. The core values increase in proportion to moral and spiritual development – it is represented through (X1, Y1) measure. If there is a rise in moral and spiritual values, core values like familyhood, common good and peace will rise. If there is a fall in the Phase 1 development, then the core values will also fall. It will lead to an increased level of crimes, conflicts, restlessness, depression, stress and many other problems.

The other part of the grid is X2 vs. Y1. If there is only Phase 2 development and Phase 1 development is neglected, then the core values decrease in proportion to phase1 development.

As Pramukh Swami Maharaj suggested to the President Dr. APJ Abdul Kalam, "Spiritual progress should be parallel to other progress." The X1 should be parallelly developed to X2.

Today, most people miss the progress on X1 and keep progressing on X2. It has led to stressful and non-satisfaction. Progress on X1 is must to maintain peace and avoid any other problems.

It is best understood through examples. In 2009, the CEO of a computer software giant company was caught for committing fraud of $1.5 billion. He was born to a farming family and earned an MBA from Ohio University, and established the company in 1987. The company went public in 1992. It also played a significant role in making Andhra Pradesh, India an IT hub. But in 2009, the fraud was exposed, and the CEO and his brother were imprisoned (Satyam_scandal, n.d.). Here we can see, the CEO's personal, intellectual, professional, emotional and social growth was excellent. But the moral growth was not strong, he collapsed. Bin Laden was highly intelligent and professional, but he caused terror and the 9/11 catastrophe. There are numerous other examples but to summarize we can say; Moral and Spiritual development is the base of Phase 2 development. Therefore, if we don't consider Phase1 development, then it will endanger peace & harmony at personal, family, organization, institution, social, national and international levels.

Complete Leadership

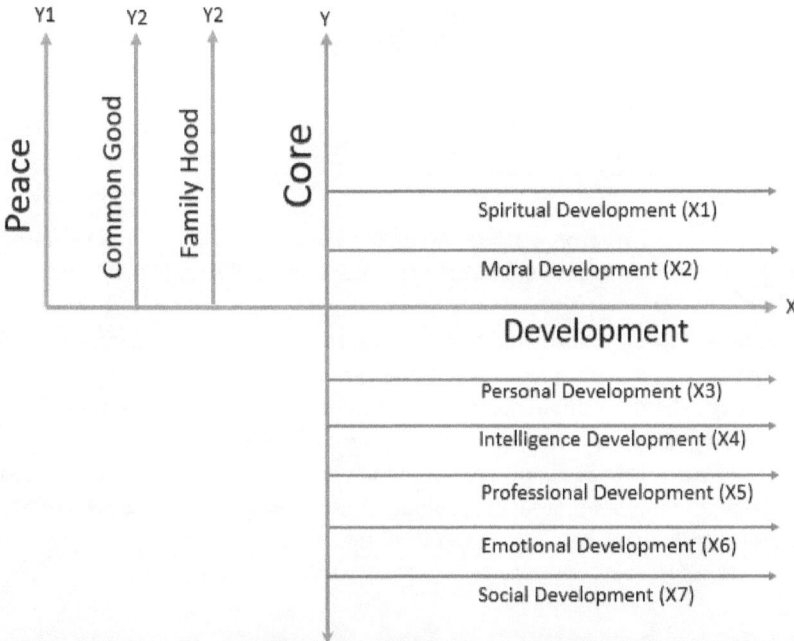

The grid here illustrates the development of seven aspects to the core of complete leadership. The seven aspects are shown separately here on the X-axis (X1 to X7) and three core values of the model on the Y-axis (Y1 to Y3). Here different combinations are possible between each X axis to Y axis. One can measure personal, family, organizational or national or international development here. The measurement should be based on the characteristics defined in the earlier sections and questionnaire. Based on this, one can judge where they need to improve to move towards completeness.

Conclusion

When we first started developing this model, we were not sure how it would come up? But it was only due to blessings of Mahant Swami Maharaj; the model evolved nicely. There are tens of thousands of incidences written in reports and books on Swamiji. We have given here only a few incidences to support and explore the Complete Leadership Model. This is just a tip of an iceberg. There is still an ocean left to explore. We had a deep sense of love and respect for Swamiji, and in respect to the leadership model, this book became a discovery of many truths about Swamiji which we invite you to discover within the pages. Swamiji truly embraced the 'Complete Leadership' style, and we are blessed to have been able to witness him in our lifetime.

Jai Swaminarayan,

BAPS Family
January 2019,
India

Email: ultimategnan@gmail.com

Bibliography

(n.d.). *Swaminarayan Bliss December 2016*.

"Depression: let's talk says WHO, as depression tops list of causes of ill health. (n.d.). Retrieved from www.who.int: https://www.who.int/news-room/detail/30-03-2017--depression-let-s-talk-says-who-as-depression-tops-list-of-causes-of-ill-health

101 Tales of Wisdom by Yogiji Maharaj. (n.d.). Retrieved 11 22, 2018, from www.exoticindiaart.com: https://www.exoticindiaart.com/book/details/101-tales-of-wisdom-as-told-by-yogiji-maharaj-IDL205/

(2012, December). *Swaminarayan Bliss, Nov-Dec* .

(2013, 11). *Swaminarayan Bliss November*.

(2016). *Swaminarayan Bliss September-October*.

Akshardham Temple Attack. (n.d.). Retrieved from https://en.wikipedia.org: https://en.wikipedia.org/wiki/Akshardham_Temple_attack#National_Security_Guards_(NSG)_pursue_and_kill_terrorists

Aksharjivandas, S. (1997). *Pure Devotion* (1st ed.). (S. Yogvivekdas, Trans.) Ahmedabad, Gujarat, India: Swaminarayan Aksharpith. Retrieved 11 10, 2018

Anandswaroopdas, S. (1998). *Divinity* (2nd ed.). (S. Paramtattvadas, Trans.) Ahmedabad, Gujarat, India: Swaminarayan Aksharpith. Retrieved 11 14, 2018

APJA Kalam, A. T. (2015). *Transcedence: My Spiritual Experiences with Pramukh Swamiji*. Harper Elements.

BAPS Swaminarayan Research Institute. (n.d.). Retrieved from www.akshardham.com: http://swaminarayanresearch.akshardham.com/about/organizer/

Bennis, W. (1998). *Managers do things right. Leaders do the right thing*. Retrieved 9 18, 2018, from https://link.springer.com/chapter/10.1007/978-3-322-82771-5_7

Bhagwad Geeta, 4/39. (n.d.).

Biography of Yogiji Maharaj. (n.d.).

Blanchard, K., & Broadwell, R. (n.d.). *Servant Leadership in Action*. Berrett-Koheler Publisher, Inc.

Blanchard, K., & Miller, M. (2014). *The Secret: What Great Leaders Know and Do*. San Francisco: Bernett-Koehier Publishers, Inc.

Bob Chapman: Why You Should Treat Your Employees As Family. (n.d.). Retrieved from forbes.com: https://www.forbes.com/sites/danschawbel/2015/10/06/bob-chapman-why-you-should-treat-your-employees-as-family/#1bdafb3f705b

Brahmopanishad. (1992). Ahmedabad, Gujarat, India: Swaminarayan Aksharpith.

cigarettes or war which is the biggest killer. (n.d.). Retrieved from https://www.theguardian.com: https://www.theguardian.com/news/reality-check/2013/dec/18/cigarettes-or-war-which-is-the-biggest-killer

Depression. (n.d.). Retrieved from www.who.int: https://www.who.int/news-room/fact-sheets/detail/depression

Divine Memories - 1 (1st ed., Vol. 1). (1997). (S. Paramtattvadas, Trans.) Ahmedabad: Swaminarayan Aksharpith. Retrieved 11 20, 2018

Divine Memories - 2 (1st ed., Vol. 2). (1997). (S. Paramtatvadas, Trans.) Ahmedabad: Swaminarayan Aksharpith.

Ego is the enemy of Good Leadership. (2018, 11). Retrieved from https://hbr.org: https://hbr.org/2018/11/ego-is-the-enemy-of-good-leadership

Eternal Virtues (1st ed.). (2009). (Y. Trivedi, Trans.) Ahmedabad: Swaminarayan Aksharpith. Retrieved 11 22, 2018

Fusion of Science and Spirituality. (2001, June 30). Retrieved from https://www.swaminarayan.org: https://www.swaminarayan.org/news/2001/06/abdulkalam/index.htm

George, B., Buhrman, R., & McLean, A. (2007, February 9). Martin Luther King Jr., A Young Minister Confronts the Challenges of Montgomery.

George, B., Buhrman, R., & McLEAN, A. N. (2007, February 9). Martin Luther King, Jr.: A Young Minster Confronts the Challenges of Montgomery. *Harvard Business School*, p. 9.

Goleman, R. (2004). *Primal Leadership: Learning to Lead with Emotional Intelligence.* Harvard Business School Press.

Guinness Book of World Records. (2002).

Guinness World Record – World's Largest Comprehensive Hindu Temple 17 December 2007. (n.d.). Retrieved from akshardham.com: https://akshardham.com/guinness-world-record-worlds-largest-comprehensive-hindu-temple-17-december-2007/

High school student punches veteran teacher in face. (n.d.). Retrieved from http://www.wmcactionnews5.com: http://www.wmcactionnews5.com/2018/11/09/high-school-student-punches-veteran-teacher-face/

Human Resource Management : A Gandhian Perspective. (n.d.). Retrieved from http://shodhganga.inflibnet.ac.in: http://shodhganga.inflibnet.ac.in/bitstream/10603/7099/11/11_chapter%203.pdf

Jeva me Nirkhya re - 6. (1995). Ahmedabad: Swaminarayan Aksharpith.

Jeva Me Nirkhya Re - 7 (Vol. 7). (1995). Ahmedabad, Gujarat, India: Swaminarayan Aksharpith.

Kjdas. (1997). *Divine Memories - 4* (1st ed., Vol. 4). (S. Chaitnyamurtidas, Trans.) Ahmedabad: Swaminarayan Aksharpith. Retrieved 11 15, 2018

Kpdas. (2009). *Pramukhcharitramrut Sagar Part 10* (1st ed., Vol. 10). Sarangpur, Gujarat, India: Sant Talim Kendra.

Kpdas. (2009). *Pramukhcharitramrut Sagar Part 11* (1st ed., Vol. 12). Sarangpur, Gujarat, India: Sant Talim Kendra.

Kpdas. (2009). *Pramukhcharitramrut Sagar Part 12* (1st ed., Vol. 12). Sarangpur, Gujarat, India: Sant Talim Kendra.

Kpdas. (2009). *Pramukhcharitramrut Sagar Part 13* (1st ed., Vol. 13). Sarangpur, Gujarat, India: Sant Talim Kendra.

Kpdas. (2009). *Pramukhcharitramrut Sagar Part 14* (1st ed., Vol. 14). Sarangpur, Gujarat, India: Sant Talim Kendra.

Kpdas. (2009). *Pramukhcharitramrut Sagar Part 15* (1st ed., Vol. 15). Sarangpur, Gujarat, India: Sant Talim Kendra.

Kpdas. (2009). *Pramukhcharitramrut Sagar Part 16* (1st ed., Vol. 16). Sarangpur, Gujarat, India: Sant Talim Kendra.

Kpdas. (2009). *Pramukhcharitramrut Sagar Part 17* (1st ed., Vol. 17). Sarangpur, Gujarat, India: Sant Talim Kendra.

Kpdas. (2009). *Pramukhcharitramrut Sagar Part 18* (1st ed., Vol. 18). Sarangpur, Gujarat, India: Sant Talim Kendra.

Kpdas. (2009). *Pramukhcharitramrut Sagar Part 2* (Vol. 2). Sarangpur, Gujarat, India: Sant Talim Kendra.

Kpdas. (2009). *Pramukhcharitramrut Sagar Part 3* (1st ed., Vol. 3). Sarangpur, Gujarat, India: Sant Talim Kendra.

Kpdas. (2009). *Pramukhcharitramrut Sagar Part 4* (1st ed., Vol. 4). Sarangpur, Gujarat, India: Sant Talim Kendra.

Kpdas. (2009). *Pramukhcharitramrut Sagar Part 5* (Vol. 5). Sarangpur, Gujarat, India: Sant Talim Kendra.

Kpdas. (2009). *Pramukhcharitramrut Sagar Part 6* (1st ed., Vol. 6). Sarangpur, Gujarat, India: Sant Talim Kendra.

Kpdas. (2009). *Pramukhcharitramrut Sagar Part 7* (1st ed., Vol. 7). Sarangpur, Gujarat, India: Sant Talim Kendra.

Kpdas. (2009). *Pramukhcharitramrut Sagar Part 8* (1st ed., Vol. 8). Sarangpur, Gujarat, India: Sant Talim Kendra.

Kpdas. (2009). *Pramukhcharitramrut Sagar Part 9* (1st ed., Vol. 9). Sarangpur, Gujarat, India: Sant Talim Kendra.

Leadership Models. (n.d.). Retrieved from www.tlu.ee: https://www.tlu.ee/~sirvir/IKM/Leadership%20Models/situational_approach.html

Lynn, A. B. (2000). *50 Activities for Developing Emotional Intelligence*. Masschussets: HRD Press, Inc.

Medcalf, J., & Gilbert, J. (2017). *Transformational Leadership*.

Moksha nu Dwar Satpurush (1st ed.). (1995). Ahmedabad, Gujarat, India: Swaminarayan Aksharpith.

Moral Disciplines. (n.d.). Retrieved from https://www.baps.org: https://www.baps.org/Spiritual-Living/Hindu-Beliefs/Moral-Disciplines.aspx

Narayancharandas. (2011). *Brahmsannidhi*. Ahmedabad: Swaminarayan Aksharpith.

Narayancharandas. (2011). *Brahmsannidhi*. Ahmedabad: Swaminarayan Aksharpith.

New York State Declares December 7th As "PRAMUKH SWAMI DAY". (2007, December 7). Retrieved Sep. 16, 2018, from http://www.swaminarayan.org/news/usa/2007/12/newyork/index.htm

Northouse, P. G. (2016). In *Leadership: Theory and Practice* (7th ed.). SAGE Publications, Inc.

Northouse, P. G. (2016). *Leadership: Theory and Practice* (7th ed.). SAGE Publications.

Opening of Swaminarayan Mandir, Selvas. (2013, July-August). *Swaminarayan Bliss*, p. 64.

Opinions. (n.d.). Retrieved from www.pramukhswami.org: www.pramukhswami.org/opinions/

Pietermaritzburg railway station. (n.d.). Retrieved from https://en.wikipedia.org: https://en.wikipedia.org/wiki/Pietermaritzburg_railway_station

PM calls temple attack well-planned conspiracy. (2002, September 25). Retrieved from https://timesofindia.indiatimes.com/: https://timesofindia.indiatimes.com/india/PM-calls-temple-attack-well-planned-conspiracy/articleshow/23294846.cms

Portrait of Inspiration (First ed.). (2002). (S. Vivekjivandas, Trans.) Ahmedabad: Swaminarayan Aksharpith.

Pramukh Charitam. (n.d.).

Pramukh Charitam. (1990). (S. A. Sadhu Brahmdarshandas, Compiler) Sarangpur, Gujarat, India.

Pramukh Gnan Sarita. (2013). Sarangpur: Sant Talim Kendra.

Pramukh Prasangam. (n.d.). Sarangpur.

Pramukh Swami among top 20 in Guiness Book. (2001, October 30). Retrieved 09 18, 2018, from https://timesofindia.indiatimes.com/city/mumbai/Pramukh-Swami-among-top-20-in-Guinness-Book/articleshow/444375939.cms

Pramukh Swami Maharaj - Life & Work in Brief (2nd ed.). (2013). Ahmedabad: Swaminarayan Aksharpith. Retrieved 11 21, 2018

Pramukh Swami Maharaj - The Inspirer and Instiller of Philosophy in Life. (2004, 12 22). Retrieved from www.swaminarayan.org: http://www.swaminarayan.org/essays/2004/2212.htm

Pramukh Swami Maharaj A Living Philosopher . (n.d.). Retrieved from www.swaminarayan.org: http://www.swaminarayan.org/essays/2004/0812.htm

Pramukh Swami Maharaj blesses Bill Clinton at Akshardham, Gandhinagar, India. (2001, April 5). Retrieved from www.baps.org: https://www.baps.org/News/2001/Pramukh-Swami-Maharaj-blesses-Bill-Clinton-at-Akshardham-1802.aspx

Pramukh Swami Maharaj:Quotes. (n.d.). Retrieved from www.goodreads.com: https://www.goodreads.com/quotes/7401385-in-the-joy-of-others-lies-our-own-in-the

Pramukh Swami's Work. (n.d.). Retrieved from www.baps.org: https://www.baps.org/About-BAPS/TheCurrentSpiritualGuru-PramukhSwamiMaharaj/His-Work.aspx

Sadhu , K. (2009). *Pramukh Charitramrut Sagar Part 1* (1st ed., Vol. 1). Sarangpur, Gujarat, India: Sant Talim Kendra.

Sadhu, P. (2001). *Vicharan Report June 2001.* Ahmedabad.

Sadhu, P. (2004, November 12). Report on Swamiji.

Sadhu, P. (2012, 05 25). Report on Swamiji.

Sadhu, V. (1992). *Brahmopanishad.* Ahmedabad, Gujarat, India: Swaminarayan Aksharpith.

Sadhu, V. (1997). *Immortal River.* (S. Paramtattvadas, Trans.) Ahmedabad, Gujarat, India: Swaminarayan Aksharpith.

Sadhuta na Sumeru. (1995). Ahmedabad: Swaminarayan Aksharpith.

Sarangpur-8: The Characteristics of Jealousy. (n.d.). Retrieved from http://www.anirdesh.com: http://www.anirdesh.com/vachanamrut/index.php?format=gu&vachno=86

Satyam_scandal. (n.d.). Retrieved from https://en.wikipedia.org: https://en.wikipedia.org/wiki/Satyam_scandal

Selected Articles about Pramukh Swami Maharaj. (n.d.). Retrieved from www.baps.org: https://www.baps.org/About-BAPS/TheCurrentSpiritualGuru-PramukhSwamiMaharaj/Articles.aspx

Sexual Assault. (n.d.). Retrieved from www.wikipedia.org: https://en.wikipedia.org/wiki/Sexual_assault

Shelat, D. K. (2017). *Yugpurush Pujya Pramukh Swami Maharaj - a life dedicated to others* (3rd ed.). Ahmedabad, Gujarat, India: Sahitya Mundranalaya Pvt. Ltd. Retrieved 11 5, 2018

Shooting of Kayla Rolland. (n.d.). Retrieved from https://en.wikipedia.org: https://en.wikipedia.org/wiki/Shooting_of_Kayla_Rolland

Socio Spiritual Works. (n.d.). Retrieved from www.pramukhswami.org: https://pramukhswami.org/work/

Son charged with murder in shooting death of father at southwest Houston apartment. (2018, 06 11). Retrieved from https://www.click2houston.com/: https://www.click2houston.com/news/son-shoots-father-to-death-during-argument-at-southwest-houston-apartment-police-say

Steve Jobs Last Words Before Death. (n.d.). Retrieved 12 04, 2018, from www.speakingtree.in: https://www.speakingtree.in/blog/steve-jobs-last-words-will-make-you-change-your-view-of-life-completely

Swami ni Vaato, 2/77. (n.d.). Retrieved from www.anirdesh.com: http://www.anirdesh.com/vato/index.php?by=prakaran&lang=gu&sortby=prakaran&prakaran=2&beg=77&increment=1

(2015). *Swaminarayan Bliss Nov-Dec.* Ahmedabad.

Swamishri Addresses the Peace Summit. (2000, September). Retrieved from www.baps.org: https://www.baps.org/Article/2011/Swamishri-Addresses-the-Peace-Summit-2094.aspx

Teachings. (n.d.). Retrieved from http://chaitanyadham.tripod.com: http://chaitanyadham.tripod.com/teachings.htm

Texas School Shooting Leaves 10 People Dead. (2018, May 19). Retrieved from https://www.abc.net.au: https://www.abc.net.au/news/2018-05-19/gunman-opens-fire-in-texas-high-school-killing-up-to-10/9778594

The Ashram Vows. (n.d.). Retrieved from https://www.mkgandhi.org: https://www.mkgandhi.org/momgandhi/chap63.htm

The 'Cockroach Theory' Of Sundar Pichai. (n.d.). Retrieved from https://toistudent.timesofindia.indiatimes.com: https://toistudent.timesofindia.indiatimes.com/news/top-news/the-cockroach-theory-of-sundar-pichai/15817.html

The Current Spiritual Guru Pramukh Swami Maharaj. (n.d.). Retrieved from www,baps.org.

The Toll of Tobacco in the United States. (n.d.). Retrieved from https://www.tobaccofreekids.org: https://www.tobaccofreekids.org/problem/toll-us

Thomas, S. (n.d.). *Statistics on Drug Addiction.* Retrieved from https://americanaddictioncenters.org: https://americanaddictioncenters.org/rehab-guide/addiction-statistics

Trait leadership. (n.d.). Retrieved 11 22, 2018, from Wikipedia: The Free Encyclopedia: http://en.wikipedia.org/wiki/Trait_leadership
Vachnamrutam Gadhada Section II. (n.d.). Ahmedabad: Swaminarayan Aksharpith.
(n.d.). *Vicharan Report 2002.* Ahmedabad.
(n.d.). *Vicharan Report 2003.* Ahmedabad.
(n.d.). *Vicharan Report April 2001.* Ahmedabad.
(n.d.). *Vicharan Report April 2001.* Ahmedabad.
(n.d.). *Vicharan Report April 2004.* Ahmedabad.
(n.d.). *Vicharan Report April 2004.* Ahmedabad.
(n.d.). *Vicharan Report April 2004.* Ahmedabad.
(n.d.). *Vicharan Report April 2004.* Ahmedabad.
(n.d.). *Vicharan Report April 2005.* Ahmedabad.
(n.d.). *Vicharan Report April 2008.* Ahmedabad.
(n.d.). *Vicharan Report April 2010.* Ahmedabad.
(n.d.). *Vicharan Report August 2004.* Ahmedabad.
(n.d.). *Vicharan Report August 2008.*
(n.d.). *Vicharan Report December 2002.*
(n.d.). *Vicharan Report February 2005.*
(n.d.). *Vicharan Report February 2005.*
(n.d.). *Vicharan Report February 2010.* Ahmedabad.
(n.d.). *Vicharan Report February 2011.* Ahmedabad.
(n.d.). *Vicharan Report January 1985.* Ahmedabad.
(n.d.). *Vicharan Report January 2001.* Ahmedabad.
(n.d.). *Vicharan Report January 2005.* Ahmedabad.
(n.d.). *Vicharan Report January 2007.* Ahmedabad.
(n.d.). *Vicharan Report July 2003.* Ahmedabad.
(n.d.). *Vicharan Report July 2004.* Ahmedabad.
(n.d.). *Vicharan Report July 2005.* Ahmedabad.
(n.d.). *Vicharan Report July 2005.* Ahmedabad.
(2011). *Vicharan Report July.* Ahmedabad.
(2012). *Vicharan Report July.* Ahmedabad.
(n.d.). *Vicharan Report June 2004.*
(n.d.). *Vicharan Report June 2005.*
(n.d.). *Vicharan Report June 2010.* Ahmedabad.
(n.d.). *Vicharan Report March 2001.* Ahmedabad.
(n.d.). *Vicharan Report March 2001.* Ahmedabad.
(n.d.). *Vicharan Report March 2008.* Ahmedabad.
(n.d.). *Vicharan Report March 2009.* Ahmedabad.
(*Vicharan Report March 2010*). Ahmedabad.
(n.d.). *Vicharan Report May 2004.* Ahmedabad.

(n.d.). *Vicharan Report May 2006*. Ahmedabad.
(n.d.). *Vicharan Report May 2007*. Ahmedabad.
(n.d.). *Vicharan Report May 2008*. Ahmedabad.
(n.d.). *Vicharan Report November 2004*. Ahmedabad.
(n.d.). *Vicharan Report November 2005*. Ahmedabad.
(n.d.). *Vicharan Report November 2005*. Ahmedabad.
(n.d.). *Vicharan Report November 2010*. Ahmedabad.
(n.d.). *Vicharan Report October 2007*. Ahmedabad.
(n.d.). *Vicharan Report September 2002*. Ahmedabad.
(n.d.). *Vicharan Report September 2002*. Ahmedabad.
(n.d.). *Vicharan Report September 2003*. Ahmedabad.
(n.d.). *Vicharan Report September 2005*. Ahmedabad.
(n.d.). *Vicharan Report September 2007*. Ahmedabad.
(n.d.). *Vicharan Report September 2008*. Ahmedabad.
(n.d.). *Vicharan Report September 2008*. Ahmedabad.
(n.d.). *Vicharan Report September 2011*. Ahmedabad.
Virkus, S. (2009). *Leadership Attributes: Trait Approach*. Retrieved from https://www.tlu.ee/~sirvir: https://www.tlu.ee/~sirvir/IKM/Leadership%20Attributes/research_on_leadership_traits.html
Vision Quotes. (n.d.). Retrieved 11 25, 2018, from www.brainyquote.com: https://www.brainyquote.com/topics/vision
Vivekjivandas, S. (2003). *Vibrations - Inspiring Incidents from Pramukh Swami Maharaj's Life* (1st ed.). Ahmedabad, Gujarat, India: Swaminarayan Aksharpith. Retrieved 11 23, 2018
Viveksagardas. (1997). *Immortal River*. (Paramtattvadas, Trans.) Ahmedabad, Gujarat, India: Swaminarayan Aksharpith.
What made Gandhiji wear only Loincloth or Dhoti. (n.d.). Retrieved from http://pib.nic.in: http://pib.nic.in/newsite/printrelease.aspx?relid=149833
Yauvan na Suhrad. (n.d.). Swaminarayan Aksharpith.

www.ingramcontent.com/pod-product-compliance
Lightning Source LLC
Chambersburg PA
CBHW030636220526
45463CB00004B/1547